Dr. Rosetta Hall's
Journal of Edith Margaret Hall
My Little Comforter

Volume 6

Rosetta Sherwood Hall

Dr. Rosetta Hall's Journal of Edith Margaret Hall: My Little Comforter
© 2017 by Esther Foundation
www.estherfoundationusa.org
1119 Old North Gate Road
Colorado Springs, Colorado USA

All rights reserved. No portion of this book may be reproduced, stored in a retrieval system, or transmitted in any form or by any means—electronic, mechanical, photocopy, recording, scanning, or other—except for brief quotations in critical reviews or articles, without the prior written permission of the author.

Preface

Dr. Rosetta Sherwood Hall was born in 1865 in Liberty, New York, the daughter of a well-to-do Christian farming family. She obtained a teacher's certificate at the age of sixteen, and after teaching at local schools for a few years, was sent in 1890 to the remote far eastern land of Korea to devote her life to medicine and missionary work under the auspices of the Woman's Medical Missionary Society of the Methodist Episcopal Church. She would go on to serve as a medical missionary there for forty-three years.

For hundreds of years, Korea had observed the 내외법 *Nae Wae Beop*, a Confucian law stipulating the strict segregation of gender. This law had restricted women's access to formal education, professional training, political representation, and movement in the public sphere. Missionaries like Dr. Rosetta Hall dedicated themselves not only to serving women who did not have access to proper medical care, but also to widely expanding these women's social opportunities and renewing their sense of self-esteem. With the heart of Christ, Dr. Rosetta Hall exercised love and compassion on Korea's underprivileged. Her significant achievements include adapting Braille into Korean script, which inaugurated a formalized education system for Korea's blind and deaf. She trained many girls and young women in the medical profession, giving them the knowledge and agency to care for their own people.

At the time of appointment, she was supposed to have served a five-year term in the field as a single missionary. Two years into her term, she married Rev. William James Hall, M.D., whom she met in the slums of New York City while they were working as medical missionaries there. Until Rev. Hall's tragic death by typhus fever in November 1894, they worked in Seoul, started work in Pyongyang, and began raising a newborn son, Sherwood.

After burying her beloved husband, Rosetta returned to New York with her infant son and a daughter in her womb. While in the States, she furthered the work she undertook in Korea. She oversaw the education of Esther Pak Kim, Korea's first female doctor of medicine, who received her M.D. degree in 1900 at the Baltimore Woman's Medical College; she raised funds and established the Hall Memorial Hospital in Pyongyang in February 1897; and she published a biography of her late husband in August 1897. It was during this time that Rosetta visited the New York Institute for the Blind and drew from New York Point to begin development of Korean Braille.[1]

She returned to Korea in 1897 with her two children to serve in Pyongyang, where she had begun pioneering mission work with her husband and had endured severe persecution. Shortly after her arrival, however, her 3-year-old daughter, Edith Margaret, died of dysentery. Rosetta suffered greatly from this loss, even more so than when she had lost her husband. She wrote in her diary a letter to her dead daughter:

> "Mamma can't help longing for a happier experience, and she has tried to lay her Isaac on the altar, and to let God do with her the best he can; and even where she may not have succeeded in this, it seems as if God himself has taken her most precious things, and she has tried to learn the lessons He would have her, and not be rebellious."

Rosetta's faith is remarkable in the face of her great personal losses. Despite her lack of understanding over their meaning, she said she "must just give her feelings over to Jesus and trust him implicitly."

In the summer of 1901, Dr. Rosetta Hall returned to New York for the second time, physically and mentally exhausted. After recuperating at the Castile Sanatorium for eight months, she again returned to Korea in the spring of 1903. Until her retirement in 1933, she remained

---

[1] The first embossed book for the blind of Korea, the syllabary and first six lessons from Mrs. George Heber Jones' 초학언문 *Chyo Hók Eun-Mun* (*A Korean Primer* - nine cards, about 5½ x 9 inches, pricked on oiled Korean mulberry paper by hand in 1897), was donated to Taegu University School of Special Education by her granddaughter Phyllis Hall King in 1996 and is currently on display at the Rosetta Hall Museum Room.

steadfast in her work. She founded the Women's Medical Training Classes in Pyongyang and Seoul; her class in Seoul would later become the Women's Medical Institute, the precursor to Korea University's College of Medicine. She established four hospitals: the Baldwin Dispensary in Seoul (1892), the Woman's Hospital of Extended Grace in Pyongyang (1894), the Hall Memorial Hospital in Pyongyang (1897), and the Chemulpo Woman's Hospital (1921). She also helped to establish the Edith Margaret Children's Wards in Pyongyang and the Child's Welfare Clinic in Seoul. Her work on behalf of the blind and deaf gained recognition throughout East Asia, leading to the Convention on the Education of the Blind and Deaf of the Far East, first held in Pyongyang in August 1914. Her forty-three years of service in Korea were a true testament to her resilience, her bravery, and her spirit. But they also testify to her religious conviction and purpose. In spite of the sacrifices she made and the losses she sustained, her obedience was drawn from the wellspring of her love for God and for the Korean people. God's provision, enacted through Dr. Rosetta Hall and many other devoted workers, liberated Korea's underprivileged—the women, the poor, and the handicapped—and privileged them anew as children of the King.

It is a blessing and an amazing grace that the work of transcribing and translating Dr. Rosetta Hall's diaries fell upon me. A faithful life is most precious in His eyes, and such a life is now able to be recorded, recognized, and passed down through the generations. I thank the Hall family for preserving and donating these diaries. The *Journal of Sherwood Hall*, in particular, passed through many hands in order to survive. Prior to his forced evacuation from Korea by the Japanese, Dr. Sherwood Hall had sent the journal to Miss Lund, who boarded the last evacuation boat to North America, the *S.S. Mariposa*. She brought it with her across the Pacific, and upon her arrival in Los Angeles, she sent it through post to Pastor Scott of Liberty, New York, to whom it arrived safely in December 1940. After Dr. Rosetta Hall's death in 1951, two generations of the Hall family—her son Dr. Sherwood Hall, his wife Dr. Marian Hall, their daughter Mrs. Phyllis Hall King, and her husband Dr. Edward King, Jr.—have preserved these diaries over the course of sixty-four years. On January 1, 2015, Dr. and Mrs. King generously decided to offer the documents to the public.

I spent three days and nights with them in their home in McLean, Virginia, brainstorming about how to best benefit the public with the history, stories, and lessons written in the diaries. I was asked to translate the diaries into Korean and publish them in both Korean and English. In April 2015, all six diaries of Dr. Rosetta Hall (four diaries from 1890 – 1894 and two scrapbooks chronicling Sherwood and Edith's childhoods) were donated to the Yanghwajin Foreign Missionary Cemetery in Seoul, where Dr. Rosetta Hall and her five other family members are buried. The first diary of 1890 was published with a Korean translation in September 2015 as a highlight for Yanghwajin's Special Exhibition commemorating Dr. Rosetta Hall's 150th birthday. The rest of the volumes will be published over the next year.

Readers of both English and Korean will benefit from these volumes. Essentially, they were her scrapbooks. Many letters, photographs, newspaper articles, sketches, and notes, as well as locks of hair, clothing, and pressed flowers and leaves, are preserved in the books as primary sources. She had continued to add notes and memo clips to her original material as the years passed by, writing around the edges and filling in the open margins. I have left her materials and texts mostly in their original state, correcting only a few spelling errors and re-arranging some of the entries to reflect their chronology.

Since her girlhood days on a farm in Liberty, New York, Dr. Rosetta Hall loved God and strained to hear His voice. In spite of doubt and tribulation, she followed Him and obeyed His commands. She went to the land where no one else would go, and she fulfilled the good work that no one else would fulfill. She loved the people no one else seemed to love. She grew from the roots of God's Love and was able to stand up again and again throughout all her storms, in order to convey that Love to others. What a great mind, and a beautiful life!

I hope for the readers of these diaries to be blessed and inspired by Dr. Rosetta Hall's example.

Sue Kim

Colorado Springs

December 4, 2015

"The Sherwood Farmhouse, Liberty, N. Y. Edith's and her mother's Birthplace."

Friday, January 18, 1895

You are the helper of the fatherless. Psalms 10:14

Ere last year's moon had left the sky,
    A birdling sought my Indian nest,
And folded, oh, so lovingly!
    Her tiny wings upon my breast.

From morn till evening's purple tinge,
    In winsome helplessness she lies;

Journal of Edith Margaret Hall

> Two rose leaves with a silken fringe,
>   Shut softly on her starry eyes.
>
> This beautiful, mysterious thing,
>   This seeming visitant from heaven,
> This bird with the immortal wing,
>   To me—to me, Thy hand has given.   —"Fanny Forester"[2]

At seven o'clock this morning, a precious little baby girl was laid in Mama's arms. Her name is Edith Margaret Hall, a name chosen long ago in Korea by her papa and mama, the "Margaret" because it is Papa's dear mother's name, and "Edith" was a favorite name with both Papa and Mama. Little Edith Margaret weighs seven and one-half pounds in her "birthday dress." Aunt Esther washed and dressed her, she was very good, crying but very little, and not at all after being nursed. My! But she is a little smacker, when she nurses, from the very first she did just as the Koreans do when they want to show they like what they are eating. Edith Margaret seems like a real strong baby. She can lift her head right up now. She is better looking than her brother when he was a little baby, but that is not saying she is pretty by any means. She has round blue eyes that stare with wonder at the strange things now about her. She has a sweet little rosebud of a mouth and prettily shaped ears. Her nose is rather large and a bit "stuck up" at present and her forehead is low, and she has not much hair on the top of her head, however, these things will no doubt all straighten out in time, and my little daughter will grow up a good looking girl.

> "'But handsome is who handsome does'
>   When heart is filled with grace
> And pleasant words are lovelier far
>   Than many a pretty face."

When Sherwood came in, he looked surprised to see a little baby in Mama's arms, but he seemed pleased, and laid his head lovingly against Mama's, and then gently patted sister's little head, and kissed her. I am sure he will love his baby sister more and more as the days and years go by, and what a dear brother he will be to Edith Margaret. Poor babe, she never saw her father, his eyes closed in death before her eyes ever opened in life. Dear Papa, how much he would like to have seen his wee little daughter, how much he would have loved her, rather how much he does love her, for he knew she was coming and remembered her when he was almost too sick

---

[2] Fanny Forester was pen name for Emily E. Judson (1817-1854). Born Emily E. Chubbuck, she married Dr. Adoniram Judson and joined him in missionary labor in Burma. This poem entitled "My Bird" was dedicated to her daughter born in Maulmain. She lost her husband not quite four years from marriage as well as her son and returned, with her daughter, to the United States and died in 1854, four year after her husband's death.

to think or to talk, and he asked about her, and smiled and seemed pleased when Mama said she thought she was going to be a strong baby. "Love is the one indestructible element in the universe," so our little daughter may be assured she has dear Papa's love, though she cannot have him until "The tabernacle of God is with men, and He will dwell with them, and they shall be His people, and God himself shall be with them, and be their God. And God shall wipe away all tears from their eyes; and there shall be no more death, nor crying, neither shall there be any more pain. Rev. xxi. 3,4.

Little Edith first opened her blue eyes in the home where her mama was born (see picture). In her papa's favorite chapter (Isaiah 43) there is one verse that reads, "Fear not; for I am with thee; I will bring thy seed from the east and gather thee from the West." And it seems strange to note that Sherwood was born in Korea in the "Far East" while his little sister not 15 months later was born ten thousand miles away in Liberty, New York.

Monday, February 18, 1895

"Edith's hair"

Leave thy fatherless children, I will preserve them alive, and let thy widows trust in me. Jer. 49:11

Just a little baby, lying in my arms, —
Would that I could keep you, with your baby charms;
Helpless, clinging fingers, "bonny brown hair,"[3]
Where the sunshine lingers, caught from other where;
Blue eyes asking questions, lips that cannot speak,
Roly-poly shoulders, dimple in your cheek;
Dainty little blossom in a world of woe,
Thus I fain would keep you, for I love you so. —Louisa Chandler Moulton

Dear Little Edith Margaret is a one month old today. "One month old, eat and sleep; precious little human heap."[4] She has been a good girl, and has gained 2 1/2 pounds, so she now weighs 10 pounds, and is 23 inches long. A bit of her "bonny brown" here is a fast and to this page. Poor little Edith, she has to wear her brother's baby clothes altogether, Mama did not make her one thing for her very own self. However, Aunt Maggie Sherwood[5] knit her a pretty pair of baby socks, and Cousin Velt[6] also send her a pair; and Mrs. Reynolds of Korea gave her

---

[3] The original words from the poem "If I Could Keep Her So" reads "downy golden hair."
[4] From "*Mother Truth's Melodies: Common Sense for Children, A Kindergarten,*" 1887, London: Forgotten Books.
[5] Mrs. Margaret Ver Noy Sherwood (Aunt Maggie) is the wife of Charles Hurd Sherwood, Rosetta's half brother.
[6] Rosevelt Rensler Sherwood (1885–1919, Cousin Velt) is the eldest son of Rev. Frank Rosevelt Sherwood, Rosetta's half brother.

mama a little package "to be opened after arriving home," and this also proved to be a pair of dainty white socks for little Edith Margaret. Also in the good steamship *China* on the way to America, Miss Laura J. Barton, a missionary upon her way home from China, knit her a pretty light blue cap. Cousin Emma Young[7] sent a handsome carriage blanket white on one side and blue on the other with a border crocheted of white. Aunt Maggie also sent some of little Cousin Fannie's[8] baby clothes, so altogether little Edith has a good supply—many of the brother Sherwood's things had not been worn at all but a very little.

Last Friday was the first that Mama went away and left baby Edith. She went to see Professor Abrams about Aunt Esther[9] going to school.[10] The Professor has a little boy named Horace who was born on the 18th of January last year, so he is just one year older than Mama's little girl. He runs alone. Edith got on so nicely without her mama; she went again the next day and took Aunt Esther as the Professor wanted to see her. Grandma took good care of her little granddaughter, and fed her some catnip tea.

Mama got a nice letter from Aunt Lillie Hall[11], Grandpa and Grandma Hall sent their love to their new grandchild.

All the accomplishments that little Edith Margaret can boast of as yet are to eat and sleep and smile. She is a good little girl sleeping most of the time and crying but little so far. She sleeps so well at night, only waking once to nurse. So far mama has had enough milk of her own for her wee daughter.

Monday, March 18, 1895

In Thee the fatherless findeth mercy. Hosea 14:3

These severe afflictions not from the ground arise. But oftentimes celestial
benedictions assume this dark disguise.   —Longfellow

---

[7] Mrs. James Chandler Young, née Emma Crary, is Rosetta's cousin Polly Burr Crary's daughter. Polly Burr Crary (1833 – 1899) is the daughter of Polly Sherwood Burr (1797 – 1878), Rosetta's paternal aunt; Polly married Horace H. Crary (1824 – 1898), a prominent businessman in tannery.
[8] Fanny Sherwood is the daughter of Mr. and Mrs. Charles Hurd Sherwood.
[9] Mrs. Esther Kim Pak.
[10] Esther Pak came to America with her husband Yousan Pak in January 1895; she entered public school at Liberty, New York, in February 1895, while her husband worked on Rosetta's father's farm.
[11] Lillie Hall is William James Hall's younger sister.

Journal of Edith Margaret Hall

Today in mama's little girl is two months old, and weighs 11 pounds; she is 24 inches long and her head 14¾ inches in circumference. She looks much larger than last month, and she smiles and coos and almost laughs out loud, and is beginning to talk "baby talk" already.

Little Edith had an attack of dysentery the first part of the month that lasted about a week. She suffered much pain, and cried very hard at times, but had only one bad night. It happened to be the first week that Aunt Esther went to school and Mama got very tired working over her dear little sick baby so much, her back has not got rested yet; but little Edith is quite well and strong again and that is so good, Mama is very thankful. I suppose having had the dysentery, and then growing an inch longer is the reason that she only weighs one pound more than last month when she looks so much larger.

Grandma Sherwood loves little Edith very much and likes to take care of her a little most every day; she kisses her and talks baby talk with her, and they get on very happily together. Edith has also sat upon Grandpa's knee two or three times and was a good girl.

Mama saw a pretty picture one morning that she would liked to have had photographed. Dear Grandma had little Edith on one knee and a great big Maltese cat on the other, while Grandpa sat close by holding Sherwood, and little dog Friskie was teasing to climb up.

Thursday, April 18, 1895

The Lord relieveth the fatherless and widow. Psa. 146:9

"How many pounds does baby weigh?
    Baby who came 'three months'[12] ago;

How many pounds from 'growing crown'[13]
    To rosy joint of the restless toe?"

    Only twelve and one-half pounds, but then

"Nobody weighed the baby's smile,
    Or the love that came with the helpless one; ++
No index tells the mighty worth
    Of a little baby's quiet breath.

---

[12] From the poem "Weighing the Baby" by Ethel Lynn Beers (1827 – 1879), Rosetta replaced "a month" to "three months" for Edith's age at this time.
[13] Rosetta replaced "crowning curl" to "growing crown."

> Nobody weighed the baby's soul,
> > For here on earth no weight there be
> That could avail; God only knows
> > Its value in eternity."[14]

Again little Edith Margaret has been quite sick with dysentery, for a whole week when she was ten weeks old. Mama used the same treatment as before—washing out the bowel with a little warm water t.i.d.[15] (about ℥ iv with Listerine ♏v)[16] and this quickly relieved the straining and pain and the frequent movements; then she ate only Horlicks Food[17] alone leaving out the cow's milk, and had Mama's milk only at night. Mama had to wean her baby girl from her milk in the day time, because Mama did not grow stronger but felt so tired every day. Edith was able to eat well and to retain her foot after the first day, and did not suffer much, so in spite of the dysentery she gained one and one half pounds. Her head now measures 15½ inches and she is 25 inches long.

On April 10th, baby Edith really laughed aloud heartily like Sherwood began to do when he was six months old. She likes to play with her baby fingers and begins to notice a tin rattle her mamma bought for her the other day, but though she will grasp it in her tiny hand she soon drops it. She is fond of company and likes someone to play with her.

She seems real well and strong now, sleeps well at night, sometimes all night long, and seldom wakens more than once. In the morning she will lie for an hour often, cooing and laughing, kicking and stretching, "as happy as a baby can be." She doesn't like to be washed though, especially the dressing part. She is often good through the bathing, but when it comes to putting on her clothes she most always cries hard like a naughty baby. Grandma sometimes makes her a "sugar teat"[18] of a cracker and Horlicks Food, and that often comforts her, but not always.

Though Mama stopped nursing Edith through the day soon after her two month's birthday, and only nurses her when she goes to sleep at night and once when she wakes up, yet Mama doesn't get rested, and her back aches so, that she has decided she better not nurse baby

---

[14] "Weighing the Baby" by Ethel Lynn.
[15] Three times a day.
[16] "About 4 ounces of water with 5 minims of Listerine." 5 minims are about 5 drops. 1 minim = 0.01616115199 milliliters.
[17] Horlicks Food is the malted milk hot drink developed by founders James and William Horlick.
[18] Sugar-teat was a popular method of feeding infants. It was prepared by mixing pulverized sugar-crackers with milk or water to form a dough, which was then put in to a linen rag and tied with a string to form a ball about the size of a small apple. This soft, sweet ball was put into the mouth of the child, when it could not be quieted by the ordinary means, at which it instantly began to suck, and thus may have been kept quiet for hours.

Edith anymore at all, and probably tomorrow will be the last time. Mama is so sorry, for Edith enjoys it so, and Mama did want to nurse her through the summer so much.

Edith had her little hood and cloak on for the first time today and had a short walk outdoors. She took a nice long sleep afterwards.

Aunt Alice Gray[19] wrote Mama a nice letter recently in which she said Grandma Hall was pleased with Edith Margaret's name.

Saturday, May 18, 1895

The Father Himself loveth you. Jn. 16:27

"Hush, my dear, lie still and slumber,
    Holy angels guard thy bed;
Heavenly blessings without number
    Gently falling on thy head.

Sleep, my babe, thy food and raiment,
    House and home, thy friends provide;
All without thy care or payment,
    All thy wants are well supplied.

Soft and easy is thy cradle:
    Coarse and hard thy Saviour lay,

When His birthplace was a stable
    And His softest bed was hay

Lo, He slumbers in His manger,
    Where the horned oxen fed:
Peace, my darling; here's no danger,
    Here's no oxen near thy bed.

'Twas to save thee, child, from dying,
    Save my dear from burning flame,
Bitter groans and endless crying,
    That thy blest Redeemer came.

May'st thou live to know and fear Him,

---

[19] Alice Hall Gray is William James Hall's younger sister.

> Trust and love Him all thy days;
> Then go dwell for ever near Him,
> > See His face, and sing His praise!
>
> I could give thee thousand kisses,
> > Hoping what I most desire;
> Not a mother's fondest wishes
> > Can to greater joys aspire."[20]

Edith Margaret is four months old now, and weighs 14 pounds, more than Sherwood did when he was five months old, and was getting short dresses made ready to start for Pyong Yang. Baby Edith is yet in long clothes, and Mama wishes to keep her so just as long as she can. Mama wants to get her picture taken this month, now that baby sister is about the same size as Sherwood when he had his first pictures.

A few days ago baby Edith took her first ride behind horses. Mama took her to Liberty and she called first on her doctor, Dr. Webster, but he wasn't home, so couldn't see how much his baby had grown; then she went with Mama to Mrs. Sandford's, where Mama had a pleasant call with her old school-mate and pupil Lizzie Naylor, now Mrs. Bruce Sandford, and Sherwood played with her little son nearly one year old. Grandma Sandford thought our Edith a fine baby, and a very good one; neither she nor her brother cried while we were gone.

Edith holds a rattle or a little bone ring in her tiny hand quite a long time now, amusing herself with it, and she will laugh over her face if you show her a doll, and will coo and talk her "baby talk to it in a very enjoyable manner.

She has been real well this month, and pretty good—often sleeps all night without awaking.

> When baby wakes of mornings,
> Then it's wake, ye people all!
> > For another day
> > Of song and play
> Has come at our darling's call!
> And, till she gets her dinner,
> > She makes the welkin ring,
> And she <u>won't</u> keep still
> Till she 's had her fill—
> > The cunnin' little thing!   —Eugene Field

---

[20] "A Cradle Hymn" by Isaac Watts (1674 – 1748).

She goes outdoors every nice day.

Tuesday, June 18, 1895

    For now we see through a glass, darkly. I Cor. xiii. 12

    "'Who'd be a mother-bird, worried all day?
Fledglings are absurd, always at play.'
I'd be a mother-bird: ah, who would not?
'Worried' is not the word, 'tis a sweet lot.
Think when her wings are spread over her nest!
Think when each little head leans to her breast!
Though then no song will come, not a note's heard,
'Tis but for joy she's dumb, glad mother-bird."

    During these four weeks that have just gone by baby Edith Margaret has been just one of the best of little girls. She eats, and sleep so well, and she awakes so happy every morning and coos and laughs and plays a long time. She has laughed out loud now heartily all the month every time Aunt Esther tries to make her, and she loves to watch her brother at play, he will amuse her a long time some days. Edith is so strong, she can almost lift herself straight up to a sitting posture, and she can sit alone quite a few minutes. She enjoys new things to play with, gets tired of the old ones. Mama gave her a rubber doll that used to be brother's that she likes quite well, also a new rattle with a lot of little bells on. She begins to like to put things in her little mouth pretty well.

    One day Mama took baby and Sherwood and Uncle Yousanie[21], and went to Liberty and spent the day at Mrs. Sarles'.

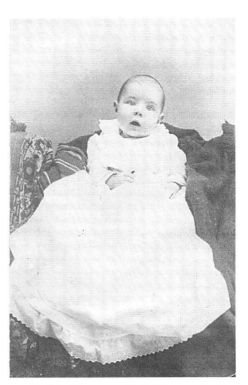

"Edith Margaret Hall 4½ months"

---

[21] Yousan Pak, Aunt Esther's husband.

Edith was such a good baby, never cried there once. They thought her the best baby they had ever seen.

Mama took baby Edith to the artists to get her picture taken; she was very happy when she went, but was suddenly taken with pangs of hunger after getting there, and Mama wanted the artist to wait till Uncle Yousanie made the food for her, and she had eaten, but the artist persisted in taking it at once between the cries, and the result is not satisfactory to Mama, she hopes she can get it done better soon.

Little Leslie Sarles quite fell in love with baby Edith, he told his mother he thought she was the nicest baby he ever saw, and he didn't see why they couldn't keep her there all the time, that Edith's mama didn't need two babies.

Edith Margaret weighs 15 pounds now, her head measures 16⅛ inches (41 cm) and she is 26 inches long. So she is larger than brother was at the same age, though somehow it doesn't seem as if she were. She is a very sunny hearted and sweet tempered as a rule, and we all love her so much.

Thursday, July 18, 1895

A merry heart doeth good like medicine. Prov. 17:22

"It gives to beauty half its power
    The matchless charm worth all the rest
The light that dances o'er the face
    And speaks of sunshine in the breast.
If beauty ne'er have set her seal
    It well supplies her absence too
And any cheek looks passing fair
    Whene'er a sunny heart shines through."[22]

Edith Margaret's six month's birthday finds her at Uncle Frank's[23] in Northville, New York. She left Liberty on the 10th with her mama and brother and Mr. and Mrs. Pak and spent two days in New York City, went one afternoon to Central Park and enjoyed a nice carriage ride. She was a good baby girl, and made but little trouble all the way to Uncle Frank's. She lived on Horlicks malted milk, but the next day after getting settled in Uncle Frank's comfortable home Mama began giving her cow's milk again. It seemed so nice there and agreed with brother all

---
[22] From "The Merry Heart."
[23] Rev. Frank Rosevelt Sherwood (1958 – 1938) is Rosetta's brother.

right, but before 36 hours had passed by she was again taken with dysentery, so Mama stopped the milk at once, and treated her as she had before, and she got all over it in three days, but when she was weighed she had lost a half pound, though she has gained an inch in length.

Just a little while before leaving Liberty, Mamma took baby Edith to another artist's and had her picture taken again, and she was so happy and good; though the artist was a long time about it, she kept so merry, and Mamma is pleased with the result; though she had bad luck in getting one of the pictures off the card and mounted in Edith's journal.

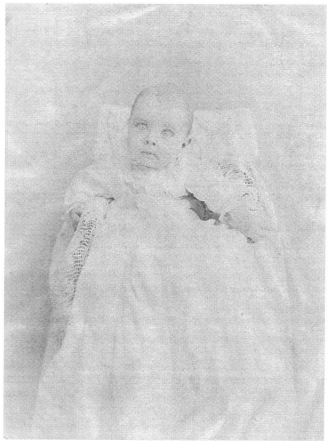

"Edith Margaret Hall 5½ months."

Three weeks ago, upon the third anniversary of Mamma's wedding day, dear Grandpa left us for his heavenly home—just the day before he kissed little Edith for the last time, and now he is with dear Papa. Poor Grandma is a so lonely without him, and so are we all—even Brother misses him—we ask him where Grandpa is and he will go and look in the bed; then he will come out and point to his empty chair; but both he and his baby sister will no doubt forget him.

Edith has enjoyed her visit at Uncle Frank's, both he and Aunt Kit[24] and Cousins Velt and Clare[25] are so kind—and Uncle Frank takes us all out riding every evening, then Edith is undressed and goes to bed and sleeps so well.

In another week we shall be on our way to Grandpa and Grandma Hall's who are eagerly waiting to see their little Korean grandchildren. Mamma trusts we shall all get there safely, and keep well. It will be rather trying to see all the dear people and visit the places that Papa loved so well without him, but no doubt he will be near us in spirit, and the God he served so faithfully will give us grace.

Sunday, August 18, 1895

Whether we live, we live unto the Lord; and whether we die, we die unto the Lord: whether we live therefore, or die, we are the Lord's. Romans 14:8

"Lord, give me grace, that I may be
Thine, with such soul-sincerity,
That, wheresoe'er my steps may move,
My first, last thought may be Thy love."[26]

This day finds baby Edith Margaret at her Grandpa and Grandma Hall's in Glen Buell, Canada. It was quite a hard day's journey here. We left Uncle Frank's at 6 a.m. and did not reach Grandpa's till 11 p.m., July 24, but Edith stood it very well, and was a good little girl. She was sleeping when she got to Grandpa's, but in the morning she got a warm welcome from all, and especially from dear Grandma.

Many people came to see little Edith and her brother and her mamma—over 100 during the first two weeks. Most of people think baby Edith resembles her Papa's people. Her eyes are so much like her Uncle John's[27], and I notice in Grandpa Hall's family of those that I have seen of his brothers and sisters, Uncle James Hall[28], and Aunt Sarah Percival[29] have similar eyes, though Grandpa Hall and Papa did not.

---

[24] Mrs. Frank Rosevelt Sherwood, née Catherine Anne MacKinlay (Aunt Kit).
[25] Clarence MacKinlay Sherwood (Cousin Clare), second son of Uncle Frank.
[26] John Samuel B. Monsell.
[27] John Hall, Dr. William James Hall's younger brother.
[28] James Hall, Dr. William James Hall's younger brother.
[29] Sarah Percival is Grandpa Hall's sister.

For while Edith was quite well, and seemed to be gaining again after her attack of dysentery at Uncle Frank's, but after she began taking about her usual quantity of cow's milk she was again taken sick, and is just now nicely getting over it. She, however, has lost a pound and now weighs but 14 pounds.

Baby Edith Margaret has made a few visits with her mamma and Grandma, and among them, she went to see her great-Grandfather Bolton at New Dublin. He is 90 years old and looks real well yet, but has been in bed over a year with a broken hip. Poor Grandpa, he is so patient. He was so pleased to see his great-grandchildren that came so far to see him, their dear Papa was a favorite with him; he used to sing, and read and play with him. The Boltons are a long lived family. Mama traced them back through the help of Grandfather Bolton and Aunt Sarah to George Bolton a United Loyalist who was born in Ireland, and there married Nancy Bickfort. They early immigrated to Canada. Upon their way in the United States, a boy baby was born to them who received the name of William[1]. He had a sister Alice who married a Mr. Carrie and lived to a great age. His brother Abram Bolton cut down a free when he was 100 years old, and he lived to be 103. There were 7 boys altogether, and but the one girl. George Bolton is buried at Lyn, and a large basswood tree has grown over his grave since that time. The son William[1] married Martha Elliott; she was of Dutch descent and was born in Vermont July 3, 1777. To them were born Sarah[1], Rebecca, John[1], Benjamin[1], Nancy and William[2]. John[1] Bolton at the age of 28 married Alice Colborne aged 23, born 1810 (died aged 75 years). To them were born six girls and three boys in the following order: Margaret (Grandma Hall), Benjamin[2] (dead), Martha (dead), Henry, Sarah[2], Susan, Jane, Caroline, and William[3] John. [illegible]. Uncle Henry, Aunt Sarah, and Uncle William[3] are unmarried and are yet home with Grandpa Bolton on the old homestead. Their stone house was built in 1835. Great-great-grandmother Martha Elliott Bolton lived here with her son John[1] until March 18, 1879 when she died aged 102 years. Papa remembered this dear old grandmother very well. She used to tell about driving off cattle from a battle field when she was 12 years old.

Though Edith has not gained any weight, but rather has lost, yet she is quite strong and has gotten so that she can sit alone nicely during the last month and she can hold her bottle with six ounces of fluid in right up straight in her two tiny hands. She looks so cunning, she is such a doll-like little creature and her feet and hands are so little, and her legs so thin. Yet she does not look sickly or puny, she goes out of doors so much that she is tanned a little, and her lips and cheeks are rosy, and she is a healthy looking baby, only small for her age. She talks a lot of baby talk, and begins to say "goi goi goi" like Sherwood used to say so much after he first came to America—Joe and Grandma used to say he said "golly golly golly" and whenever they wanted him to say it they would start him off on that word; so Aunt Ester, does the same to Edith, of course Aunt Esther doesn't know that isn't a nice word,[30] and the other day when Mamma wasn't here, Rev. and Mrs. Perley of Lyn, called, and Aunt Ester was showing the baby off to them, and she told little Edith to say "golly, golly, golly." Of course the good minister and his wife were quite shocked, and Mrs. Perley said, "Why you must not teach her to say such words"—But Aunt Esther doesn't know yet, what was the matter with it. (Unto the pure all things are pure.)[31]

Wednesday, September 18, 1895

But now, O Lord, Thou art our father; we are the clay, and Thou our potter; and we all are the work of Thy hand. Isa. 64:8

"In slumber sweet my baby lies,
    My bonny babe, my treasure!
Closed, for a time her laughing eyes
    To every earthly pleasure;
While Dreamland visions bright appear,
    And Dreamland's music charms her ear.

Backward her little head inclines
    That when she shall awaken,
The light that in her blue eyes shines
    Straight from the skies be taken;
Slowly she'll come to earth once more,
    Sailing from Dreamland's wondrous shore."

This day finds baby Edith at Cousin Polly Crary's[32] in the city of Binghamton, New York, but she will leave today for Cousin Seth Bonney's[33] in the city of Scranton, Pennsylvania.

When she left Canada two weeks ago, Grandma Hall gave her a beautiful delicate blue cashmere dress to make up for her next summer, and Aunt Alice Gray gave her material and lace for some pretty white aprons. The dear friends in Canada were all very kind to us and we wished that we might stay longer with them, but Uncle Charley[34] was anxious we should visit them as soon as possible on account of dear Cousin Lena[35] who is not likely to live long, and

---
[30] "golly" originated in the 18th century as a euphemism for God.
[31] Titus 1:15.
[32] Polly Burr Crary is Rosetta's paternal cousin (Aunt Polly Sherwood Burr's daughter). See footnote 6.
[33] Seth Bonney is Rosetta's maternal cousin (Aunt Elizabeth Gildersleeve Bonney's son).
[34] Charles Hurd Sherwood, Rosetta's brother, was a lawyer.
[35] Lena Sherwood is Charles Hurd Sherwood's daughter.

then Mama wants to get Aunt Esther in the Nursery and Child's Hospital in New York City before October 1st.[36] We will hope to go back to Canada some day when Edith is big enough girl to know more about it, and in the meantime we shall hope that some of the dear friends from that "Land of the Maple Leaf" will come to see us.

Baby Edith has been quite well now since her last birthday, and has gained the pound she lost, so she weighs 15 pounds just the same as when she left Liberty. No. 1 shoes are yet too large for her dear tiny little feet, but she is growing fast now every day, and perhaps before we get home Grandma Sherwood will think her baby girl has grown some after all. She uses condensed milk while we are traveling.

Mama's birthday will be tomorrow. She will be just 30 years old, and she was in hopes she might spend that day with her mother, but will not be able to now.

Mama's baby girl has not changed much during these last two months, but as she is in short clothes she looks some different. Her sweet little picture taken in the group on the next page gives a very good idea of baby Edith now.

Friday, October 18, 1895

For I know whom I have believed, and I am persuaded that He is able to keep that which I have committed unto Him against that day. II Tim. 1:12

"May Life to you, my baby dear,
    Be full of love and pleasure,
And earnest work that gives us here
    A foretaste of the treasure
Which you, God grant, in Heaven may store
    To deck your crown forever more."

Baby Edith Margaret is nine months old today, she is 27 inches long, and weighs 20 pounds! Isn't that good?—has gained 5 pounds since she left Canada.

---

[36] Esther Kim Pak entered the Nursery and Child's Hospital of New York City in September 1895, where she was able to earn her way for over a year and at the same time receive tutoring in Latin, physics and mathematics. She entered the Woman's Medical College of Baltimore ("Johns Hopkins") on October 1, 1896—the first Korean woman to take up the study of Western medicine. *With Stethoscope in Asia: Korea*, p161.

Journal of Edith Margaret Hall

This day finds her home at Grandma Sherwood's who sometimes claims her for her little girl, and says she "is not Rosetta's baby at all," and so Mama ran away for a week and wasn't even home on this month's birthday. She attended the Annual Meeting of the New York Branch of the W. F. M. S. which met in Brooklyn, October 16-18th. She was very kindly entertained by Mrs. John Traslow on Brooklyn Avenue, and afterwards called on some good friends of Papa's, Dr. Caldwell and Mrs. Parker on Henry Street, and staid over Sunday with Mr. and Mrs. Clayton on Bleecker Street, New York City. All the friends were anxious to know about dear little Edith and her brother. They were both real good while Mama was gone, were not sick, and Uncle Yousanie took care of them all right. Mama saw dear Aunt Esther who has taken care of little Edith so much; she is quite well; she assists the head nurse in the baby's ward of the

"At N. Y. City, September 27, 1895"

hospital where there are 47 little babies. She also is studying Latin, arithmetic, and physics, and says she thinks Latin is easier than English. She hopes to be able to enter the Woman's Medical College of Pennsylvania next year, and when she graduates she will go back to Korea as a medical missionary and Mama believes she will do great good among her people. If Mama never goes back to Korea herself, she will feel she is yet accomplishing some work there through helping Aunt Esther and Uncle Yousanie.

Edith doesn't creep yet, but she gets down in position for it now without crying (like she did at first whenever she found herself on her hands and knees) and she will likely creep in another week or so. Her first wee pearl appeared October 1st, and now she has two lower incisors.

She begins to know where her shoes and stockings and clothes belong, and tries to help put them on sometimes. Also begins to play "peek-a-boo" with Mama's handkerchief, and to try to comb her hair. Her No. 1 shoes have gotten too small at last, and Mama has laid them away for her to see when she gets a big girl—they are so cunning, they look just about right for a doll—Mama got them in Brockville, Canada. Then the three tiny pairs of black wool stockings with their pink and blue and old gold silk toes and heels that came from California have to be put away too, and larger ones that Mama got in New York City, when she was down, put on; and so Mama's baby girl grows and grows, and before Mama knows it she will be a baby no longer.

> "This is only a little girl;
>   But how does she grow? Does anyone know?
> With her hair of gold and her teeth of pearl,
>   From a baby so wee she will grow to be
> A maiden as fair as a blooming rose;
>   But no one can say, as day follows day,
> How a blade of grass or a little girl grows."

Monday, November 18, 1895

Behold, thou art fair, my beloved, yea, pleasant. Solomon's Song 1:16

> "I 'am glad my darling is' with me today
> Her smile is so bright and her heart is so gay;
> She fills all the house with her innocent glee,
> She loves her 'mama'—that's sufficient for me.
>
> She cannot yet walk, though her feet are so fair,
> They are fit for an angel or Cupid to wear;
> She cannot yet talk, though her innocent prattle
> Is sweeter and truer than most 'people's' tattle.
>
> She wakes in the morning as pure and as bright
> As a sunbeam sent forth from the fountains of light;
> And her infantile voice hums a sweet little song
> That tells of her happiness all the day long."[37]

Miss Edith Margaret is now ten months old—has gained another pound in weight and another inch in length, and her head is 17½ inches in circumference. She is practically the same size as Sherwood was at the same age, but she has only two teeth, while he had six. She however has learned to creep better than he did at ten months. She can creep away from the sitting room through Grandma's bedroom into the dining room. She uses her knees and not her feet as Sherwood used to, and those dear little dimpled knees get so red, and almost blistered.

---

[37] Anonymous. Words in the quotation marks ("am glad my darling is," "mama," and "people's") were modified from the original poem.

Journal of Edith Margaret Hall

Wednesday, December 18, 1895

Glory to God in the highest, and on earth peace, good will to men. St. Luke 2:14

"Hang up the baby's stocking
Be sure that you don't forget
The dear little dimpled darling
Has never seen Christmas yet!

Ah, what a tiny stocking!
It doesn't take much to hold
Such little toes as baby's
Safe from the frost and the cold.

But then, for the baby's Christmas,
It will never do at all
For Santa wouldn't be looking
For anything half so small.

I know what we'll do for the baby;
I've thought of a first-rate plan:
I'll borrow a stocking of Grandma—
The longest that ever I can.

And I will hang it close by brother's'[38]
Right here in the corner,—so;
And write a letter for baby,
And fasten it on the toe.

Old Santa Clause, this is a stocking
Hang up for our baby deer;
You never have seen our darling;
She has not been with us a year.

But she is a beautiful baby!
And now, before you go,
Please cram this stocking with presents,
From the top of it down to the toe."[39]

Another month has rolled about with its changes, and now the month that the Christ-child came in is here, and in a few days baby Edith will receive her first Christmas presents.

---

[38] Rosetta modified this line from the original, which reads, "And you'll hang it by mine, dear mother."
[39] "Hang Up the Baby's Stocking" by Emily Huntington Miller.

Uncle Frank has sent a Christmas box to Sherwood and Edith containing a number of nice toys that Cousins Velt and Clare want Mamma's babies to have. For Edith there is a nice picture book of muslin *The ABC of Animals*, and a nice box of blocks. Then Mamma has redressed her rag-doll which she has not had to play with her for a couple of months now, so it will be quite as good as new, and Mama can just imagine how she will hug it and pat it bye-bye. Dear Aunt Maggie remembered baby Edith too, and crocheted her a pretty blue ball trimmed with yellow, and Aunt Emma will send her a new gingham dress which Cousin Eva has worked prettily with brown. So Mamma thinks Grandma's stocking will be none too large to hold all these nice things for her darling.

Edith Margaret has not gained any weight during the last month. She has been creeping so much, and on December 1st already she began to climb up by chairs, and walk about by them and the lounge, and the doors. She is very active, and only takes one nap through the day, and sometimes that is not very long. She weighs 21 pounds, is 30 inches long and her head measures 18 inches in circumference. She seems to grow even if she doesn't weigh anymore, and she is now wearing the same winter dresses and aprons that brother wore all last winter, and they don't seem too large for her. She is outgrowing her stockings again, and her No. 2 shoes, and Mamma will soon put on her the pair of No. 4's which was the first brother outgrew, he wore them until we reached Grandpa's last winter when he was fourteen months old.

Baby Edith is quite as fond of books as her brother used to be, and leaves them with her little thumb and fore-fingers much the same; but she is not quite so careful. Mamma has not taken so much pains to teach her not to tear books as she did Sherwood, and Yousanie and Grandma often lets her tear paper to keep her quiet. The other day Mama was gone to town and Yousanie was ironing, and baby was so quiet for a long time that Grandma went to see what she was doing, and there she had Mama's a new book *The Personal Life of David Livingstone* and had torn three leaves out of it! That is the only time she has really done any damage as yet.

Edith is a great little girl to hug Mamma. When she picks her up in her arms Edith will put her little arms about Mamma's neck and lay her head over Mamma's heart and just hug her almost like Papa used to do. She and brother play real nice sometimes, but often they don't agree very well. In the morning when they first wake up before they are dressed they often play together very good-natured for long time. Edith always sleeps lying in the knee chest position now. She sleeps with Mamma, except sometimes brother's teeth bothers him so much he can't sleep in his crib, then Mama has but baby sister there and she has slept well all night. She generally does sleep good at night and awakes so happy and playful by daylight in the morning. She will sit right up in bed, and then reach out her hand to Mama's face and wake her up, and then play about the bed until Yousanie brings her bottle of warm milk. She takes 6 ounces of milk, 3 ounces of water, and about 3 ounces of lime water now. Since last month she had quite a serious attack of cholera-infantum[40]. One evening Sherwood took away her milk bottle, and gave her his apple instead, and it is surprising what she can do with those two little teeth of hers. Before anyone noticed it, she had it most all down, skin, core and all! That night she was very restless, and the next evening she would vomit a great flood, and have such big watery movements all at the same time—had to change her clothes from top to toe twice, and she didn't get well till Mama gave her a good dose of Syrup of Figs and washed out her bowel beside—quite a lot of apple skin and core passed her, for a day or two she didn't want to eat much, but she soon got all well again, but Mama began putting lime water in her milk then instead of oatmeal gruel, and she seems to be doing nicely, so have kept it up.

Since Mama last wrote in baby's journal November 18th, she has lived over again dear Papa's last week with her. He came home from Pyong Yang Monday morning November 19th and went away to Heaven Saturday evening November 24th, 1894. This year dear Grandma was taken sick that very week, and her temperature went up to 105° and it quite frightened Mama, she began to fear she was not only going to lose dear Papa and Grandpa, but Grandma too all within one year, but the dear Lord saw fit to spare her to us yet longer and blessed the treatment to her good, and she slowly began to improve, so that after ten days she was able to sit up again.

Aunt Esther wrote she was sorry to learn of dear Grandma's illness and wished she could help Mamma with nursing her, then wrote about dear Papa thus, "I just think about a year ago November this very day, I was very sad to see my dear friend and also brother in Christ leaving his dear wife and little boy, and ready to enter the pearly gates. I was so restless last night thinking about you and my dear brother who has gone away. I know how you feel, and it gives me deep sorrow to see you alone with the two dear little ones. I hope I shall be your comforter. I know you have the Holy Comforter, but I hope I can be a little comfort to you, my precious sister." Was not that a kind and thoughtful letter from baby Edith's Korean Aunt?

That Saturday evening this year Mama felt like writing a little memorial article about dear Papa's last six days at home for the "Medical Missionary Record" that Dr. Dowkoutt publishes—so many of Papa's intimate friends read that. In brother's journal is a very full account of Papa's sickness and last days with us, but as there is nothing in his little daughter's journal, Mama will now copy here the most of what she wrote that night.

Papa was taken sick at Pyong Yang, one-hundred-eighty miles from home, and the home-journey consumed over a week. Just the day before reaching home coming up the Han River in a Korean boat, Papa said in conversation with Mr. Moffett that he had been willing to leave the

---

[40] Cholera-infantum is an inflammatory disorder of the alimentary canal of the infants. It can be caused by infection but also by overfeeding and feeding wrong foods.

home-land when the Master called him to the foreign field, to leave Söul when he was called to Pyong Yang, and that he was willing and ready to go to other service on high if the Master called him from earth. After Mr. Moffett had read a chapter from the Bible and prayed with him, Papa remarked, "How sweet it is to trust in Jesus" and then he fell asleep, the first really refreshing sleep he had since his illness began.

Monday morning, November 19, just as Mamma was getting some medicine ready to visit an outpatient, word came that dear Papa had arrived. Mama hastily picked up brother, and ran to meet him. He was too sick to stand alone even, and had to be carried to his bed. Nearly his first words were, "I have known what a joy wife and home are in health, now I am to experience what a comfort they are in sickness." He seemed so bright and cheerful that first day after getting home, that it was difficult to realize he was so dangerously ill, yet the fever thermometer would register 105°. He was able to help himself some that night, but by the next he was as helpless as a babe.

Wednesday morning, Papa asked Mr. Noble to bring pencil and Papa gave him the items of expense in the trip he had just made, all his other accounts, he said, would be found in his books. He was ever thus careful about all business details. When he had finished he said, "Now, I am ready to live or to die. I would like to work here longer for the Master if it be His will, but if not, I shall go 'sweeping through the gates' 'washed in the blood of the lamb.'" Then after a moment's pause he added, "It is all the blood of Jesus."

Already it was hard for him to talk and beginning to be difficult to understand what he said—a gradually spreading paresis seemed to be involving the muscles of his throat.

Thursday morning, Papa asked for pencil and paper and attempted to write, but found that he was far too weak. This seemed to be his only trouble that he could not tell all that was in his heart to say. His eyes would look sorrowfully into Mamma's but he could only stammer brokenly, "I— love—you." In the afternoon, he asked for Sherwood, he looked at him lovingly and longingly, but he who was known in both America and Korea as the "Children's Friend" had to take a silent farewell of his only son.

His last attempt to talk much was to tell Mamma not to regret his going to Pyong Yang, and he said, "I did it for Jesus' sake and He will reward me."

Dear Papa, his faith was ever as simple as that of a child's, and he never had any more fear of death, than a babe of falling asleep in its mother's arms. Saturday, November 24, 1894, just at sunset, with both hands clasped in Mamma's and his eyes fixed so brightly upon hers, he fell "asleep in Jesus" to awake in the eternal Sabbath-day.

The next day, Sunday, his dear mortal body was laid at rest on the green banks of the river Han.

When Papa attended high school at Athens, Canada, there were beside himself two other William Jameses—William James Hayes and William James Crummy, through Papa's instrumentality these two William Jameses were converted, and while preparing for the ministry, died, William James Hayes in his second year at Drew Theological Seminary. In his memory Papa presented the Glen Buell Sunday School which they had attended as boys together, a library of 120 volumes, and on the church walls he erected a marble tablet. When Papa learned of the death of the other Williams James he wrote to Cousin Rebecca Rowsom, "I was greatly shocked to hear of the sudden death of William James Crummy. How often we are reminded that this is not our abiding home. I spent the last Sunday I was home with William James Crummy, heard him preach,—William James Hayes, William James Crummy and myself were together, and as we parted that night we knelt in Mr. Hayes' yard and had a prayer-meeting. Little did we think it would be our last. Our next will be a praise meeting."

And I heard a voice from heaven saying unto me, Write, Blessed are the dead which die in the Lord from henceforth: Yea, saith the Spirit, that they may rest from their labours; and their works do follow them. Rev. 14:13

Saturday, January 18, 1896

The day is Thine, the night also is Thine: Thou hast prepared the light and the sun. Thou hast set all the borders of the earth: Thou hast made summer and winter. Ps. 74:16, 17

Sweet little maid with winsome eyes
  That laughs all day 'beneath a forehead fair,'[41]
Gazing with baby looks so wise
  Over the arm of the oaken chair;
    Dearer than you is none to me,
      Dearer than you there can be none;
    Since in your laughing face I see
      Eyes that tell of another one.

Here where the firelight softly glows,
  Sheltered and safe and snug and warm
What to you is the wind that blows,

Edith's 1-year-old lock of hair

---

[41] Changed from "through the tangled hair" to "beneath a forehead fair."

Driving the sleet of the winter storm?
  Round your head the ruddy light
    Glints on the gold from your tresses spun,
  But deep is the drifting snow tonight
    Over the head of the other one.

Hold me close as you sagely stand
  Watching the dying embers shine;
Then shall I feel another hand
  That 'once clasped'[42] this hand of mine;
  Sing while you may your baby songs,
    Sing till your baby days are done;
  But, oh, the ache of the heart that longs
    Night and day for the other one!

—Adapted from "The Other One," Author unknown[43], a poem of four verses. R.S.H.

One whole year God has spared Mamma's baby girl to her. May He graciously add many years more! What a comfort she has been, and will be to her mamma's wounded heart. Mamma doesn't know how to thank God enough for the two dear children He, with such loving fore-thought, sent her. She prays that they may grow up to love and serve the God of their father, and thus always be "mother's comfort."

The ground is covered with snow and the men are working in the ice just as a year ago today when baby Edith Margaret first opened her blue eyes upon this world.

Aunt Emma and little Walter[44] came up then spent the day, and Cousin Nellie[45] was also here. She brought Edith a little china doll. Mamma put on Edith her pretty scotch plaid gingham that she and Grandma made this week for her. It has a ruffle over each shoulder that Edith thinks is very fine. When Sherwood came near her, she grabbed each of these ruffles and held them down tightly she was so afraid he might take them away from her. Aunt Annie got her a box of Graham crackers for her birthday,

Edith Margaret Hall, age 1

---
[42] Changed from "nestled once" to "once clasped."
[43] "The Other One" by Harry Thurston Peck.
[44] Walter Sherwood, Jr. is Rosetta's brother Walter Hill Sherwood's son.
[45] Nellie Sherwood (b. 1883) is Aunt Emma's daughter. Aunt Emma is Rosetta's brother William Fanton Sherwood's wife.

and Mamma got her a pair of shoes, 3½, those 4's of brother's did seem so large, these new ones are plenty large enough for her to grow in for some time. Edith was a good girl all day playing about by herself and watching Sherwood and Walter play. At noon, she went to sleep and slept three hours, and then she sat up till 9 o'clock this evening playing with the chips in the pan by the stove.

Ever since Christmas, Mamma's baby has crept up stairs alone nearly every day, and she is beginning to learn to creep down backward. She walks about by the chairs and the side of the house a great deal, and yesterday and today she has stood quite a few moments all alone, and she does look so cunning. She takes 7 ounces of milk and 2 ounces of water with a little lime water now five times in 24 hours. She also eats 2 baked apples every morning, and graham cracker or two during the day, and a soda cracker or a little bread and butter every night but she has only two teeth yet. Mama thinks it very strange she doesn't get more. She has gained 2 pounds this last month and now weighs 23 pounds, is 29½ inches long standing, and 31 inches lying down. Her head measures 18 inches in circumference. She has not very thick hair, but it is growing quite long now. Mamma tried to outline her hand, but she didn't hold very still, but it does quite well. It is too large however. Edith is quite inclined to be left-handed. Mama tries to break her of it all she can. She is quite as fond of putting ribbons or carpet rags about her neck for neckties as Sherwood used to be at her age, also to take bits of paper or spools or nuts out of a box and put them back, out and in amusing herself with them for a long time.

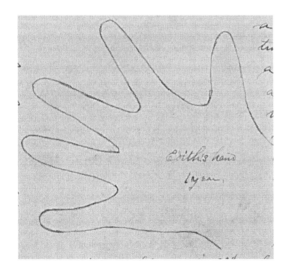

"Edith's hand 1 year"

"Kiss her once for the year that is done,
And once for the year that is just begun,
And softly sing—
'The years that are coming so fast—so fast—
Each brighter and happier be than the last;
And every hour that goes hurrying past,
New gifts to my baby bring!'"

Edith Margaret has not called "mamma" nearly so much this last month. She tries to say "bow-wow" when the dog barks and attempts to say "kitty." When she hears a wagon going by, she will creep to the window and pull herself up on her tiptoes and peek out. She loves to go outdoors and goes nearly every day when not too cold. Recently, she has begun to say "By, by" when she goes away. She will make-believe read quite long stories from a paper or book, and thinks she has to help Mamma read her letters. Grandma has been trying to teach her where her new shoes are, but has not succeeded yet. She doesn't seem to understand so much of what is said to her as Sherwood did when a year old; about the only thing she is sure to respond to is when anyone asks her to read a nice little story when she has a book or paper in her hand. She is quite different in disposition from Sherwood. She can't bear to have ointment or glycerine or anything put upon her face or lips, while he used to like it, even if Mamma put it on an applicator and inserted it up his nostrils; he was always so good to have his napkins changed, would try and lie down upon the spread out napkin himself, and seemed never in a hurry but would lie quietly while Mamma would go out in the other room to get water to wash him or anything, but Edith can't bear to spend time to have her napkins changed, and kicks, often cries, and is scrambling to get up all the time. She seems naturally of a little quicker temperament than her brother; but after all, in many things she is as patient as a little lamb, for instance when they are getting ready to go outdoors, Yousanie always fixes Sherwood up first, but if Edith only sees her hood and cloak there ready to be put on, she is quite content to wait till brother's coat, hat, mittens, and rubbers have all been adjusted. She also seems rather more affectionate of disposition than her brother, she is a great one to hug Mamma, and she is just beginning to learn to kiss. Altogether she is a very sweet little rosebud, and a great comfort to Mamma, and all the household loves her dearly. She seems an especial favorite of Joe's. May God bless her, and may she be always His very own, and help to win others for Jesus.

Sunday, February 2nd. Mama is going away tomorrow, and will be away from her darlings probably until after baby Edith's next birthday. Edith has taken a few steps alone already, and she has been saying "mamma" more of late, and has added "how d'y" to her little vocabulary. Mamma prays that she and her brother may be kept safe and well till Mamma comes home again. God bless their dear little hearts.

Wednesday, March 18, 1896

> Let thine heart keep my commandments; for length of days and long life and peace shall they add to thee. Prov. iii. 1,2
>
> So—so the days go fleeting
>   Like golden fancies free,
> And every day that cometh
>   Is full of sweets for me;
> And sweetest are those moments

Journal of Edith Margaret Hall

>   My darling comes to climb
> Into my lap to mind me
>   That it is kissing time. 　　　　　—Eugene Field

  Baby Edith Margaret is now 14 months old—just about the same age brother was when it's his sister came. She is just about the same size he was at that age, though it doesn't seem so. She weighs 25 pounds with her clothes on, is 30½ inches tall standing, and her cranium measures 18½ inches. Lying down she is 32 inches long and undressed weighs 24 pounds. Edith has cut four new teeth. They came all about the same time one month ago; she now has her four lower incisors and the two middle upper ones. Since she was 13½ months old she has given up creeping, and walks entirely now, so is six weeks ahead of her brother in that, and he did not walk till he was 15 months old. She got at it so differently from him though. He never walked of any consequence by chairs and the side of the house, but waited till he could get right up in the middle of the floor alone, and then he would start off. Edith began by climbing up by the side of a chair or by the door or wall, and for several weeks walked by taking hold of something. She would walk the whole length of the hall with her hands upon the wall, then she began trying to go alone from one chair to another or from one person to another, if she fell down she would creep till she could get hold of something to pull herself up. She but recently began to try to get right up alone like Sherwood did from the first. She was not very firm upon her feet at first and walked rather sideways as she had learned to from taking hold of things, but now she is firmer, and doesn't often fall. She does look so cunning. She has a peculiar gait, sort of a tiddle-toodle, widdle-waddle like Irish folks sometimes walk. She holds her little hands out to help balance her, but is getting so now she can walk nicely with her hands full. She was a proud, happy little girl when she first began walking alone. Sherwood hardly knew what to make of it—he had gotten quite a notion of creeping to keep her company, but now he doesn't have to anymore. Poor Mamma, she will soon have no more baby, Edith is growing up so fast. She likes to come to Mamma and put her hand on her knee, and with little coaxing grunts she will stretch herself up until Mamma lifts her, and then sometimes like Mr. Field's baby she will remind Mamma that it is "kissing time." She is a great smacker, but often times when kissing other people, especially, she gives quite "aseptic kisses" smacking again and again without touching her lips to the face. Sherwood is quite a hand to do that too; but often to Mamma they give very sweet, warm, loving kisses right on her lips or cheeks, and Edith will put her little arms around Mamma's neck and add one of her dear hugs.

  Grandmother has taught Edith where her teeth are, she will ask her "where are your little toothies?" and Edith will open her mouth wide and sometimes take hold of them, she also knows where her shoes are; and she knows very well when anyone is going away, or she goes out, to say "by by."

"When baby goes a walking
Oh, how her paddies fly!
    For that's the way
    The babies say
To other folk 'by-by.'"

Edith will also say "how d'y" like the folks down South, and she says "bow, wow, wow" very plainly whenever she hears a dog bark. She calls "kitty" and "mamma" and "Ba-ba" for Grandma, and "Dah"[46] like Sherwood does, and she is beginning to say "she-ee" when she wants to use the chamber. She uses her little chamber chair every morning early, and scarcely ever soils her napkins now.

When Mamma came home from New York and Middletown after being gone over two weeks that time she brought Edith a pretty knit doll, and Sherwood a mouth organ; Edith soon learned to play on the mouth organ too— that was a month ago. She makes just as good music as anyone that does not play a tune. She doesn't care very much for a doll yet, though if she doesn't have it too often, when she first sees it she will kiss it, and hold it in her arms and pat it, singing "bye-bye." She is fond of looking at picture books. She knows that flowers have a nice odor, and now when she sees pictures of them she will make-believe smell like Sherwood used to.

Edith loves to stand up in Sherwood's little rocking chair, taking hold of the back firmly. She will rock and rock very hard, swinging backward and forward as she goes—we have to look out for her that the chair does not tip over. She enjoys herself this way for most half an hour every evening—it makes very good exercise for her. She continues to go to bed just about 12 m.[47] every day with her bottle of milk and take a 2 hours nap. This and when she goes to sleep at night are the only times she has the bottle. When she comes downstairs in the morning she gets the most of a soft boiled eggs with cracker crumbs in it, and about 10:30 a.m. she gets a lunch of apple-sauce also mixed with cracker crumbs in it, and at 4 p.m. bread and milk, or rice, or crackers and milk or custard. Then at our supper time she sits in her little high chair at the table and eats little bread and butter, or mashed potato or something of that sort. She is much more of a hand to eat everything that is given her than Sherwood ever was.

Edith is cutting two more teeth—the upper lateral incisors, one has just cut through the gum, but the other one has not yet—that will make all of her incisors; her lower canines seem to be on the way also, and she has some quite fretful spells now like Sherwood used to. She gets

---

[46] Sherwood calls Uncle Yousanie "Dah."
[47] 12 m. is noon (midday, *meridies* in Latin).

pretty well tired out by the close of day, and is often ready to go to bed at 6 o'clock, and Sherwood goes before 8 o'clock.

> The first train starts at 6 p.m.
>   For the land where the poppy grows;
> The mother dear is the engineer,
>   And the passenger laughs and crows
>
> The palace car is the mother's arms;
>   The whistle a low, sweet strain;
> The passenger winks and nods and blinks
>   And goes to sleep in the train.
>
> At 8 p.m. the next train starts
>   For the Poppy Land afar
> The summons clear falls on the ear:
>   "All aboard for the sleeping-car!"
>
> But what is the fare to Poppy Land?
>   I hope it is not dear.
> The fare is this—a hug and a kiss—
>   And 'tis paid to the engineer.
>
> So I ask of Him who children took
>   On His knee in kindness great:
> "Take charge, I pray, of the trains each day
>   That leave between six and eight."[48]
>
>   —Edgar W. Abbott

Monday, May 18, 1896

And now abide faith, hope, love, these three; but the greatest of these is love. I Cor. 13:13

"Who rules the house with gentle sway?
And makes the proudest 'one'[49] obey?'
And serve her in the humblest way?
    The Baby.

---

[48] The title of the poem is "Poppy-Land Express."
[49] Rosetta changed "wretch" to "one."

Like stars from heaven her blue eyes beam,
She bears herself with upright mien;
O, who would wish a fairer queen
    Than Baby?

To thee, let proud man come, my dove,
He'll learn this truth that's from above,
'He rules supreme who rules by love'
    Like Baby"[50]

Our baby is now 16 months old, and a big girl she is growing to be. She is 31½ inches tall, a half inch taller than her brother was at the same age; she weighs 26 pounds so is not quite so fat as he was (28 pounds) then.

Sherwood calls her "baby" altogether now, so the rest of us generally do too, and somehow it seems as if she were more of a baby than her brother was at the same age, but, she really is not, she is rather more developed. She talks more, has added "cakee" and "ta-te" and "happy-day" to her vocabulary, and Grandma has taught her so she knows well, and will point out when asked, her nose, eyes, mouth, ears, tongue, teeth, hair, hands, feet and knees, which Sherwood did not learn till he was past 16 months old. The only thing Mamma thinks of now that baby does not do that brother did is to go <u>down</u> stairs alone, she has climbed <u>up</u> stairs ever since Christmas time, but doesn't undertake to go down yet. Edith is also weaned from milk in the bottle since the first of this month—Mama took it away from both Sherwood and Edith the same time. Edith will eat a good supper, and then just before she gets ready to go to bed will drink a whole large cup of new milk, then she has nothing more till morning and sleeps all night long as a rule. However, Mama yet allows them both their empty bottles when they go to bed at night. They are rocked to sleep without the bottle for their nap in the day, but at night nothing seems to please them better after a good drink of milk than to lay each down in their bed with their old friend, the bottle. They are both soon off to dreamland with no more trouble, and if they do awake in the night they feel around till they find the bottle, and are soon off to sleep again. Mamma ought to take it away from both, but it is so easy, and they enjoy it so well, that as yet she has not done it.

Ever since Edith was 15 months old, she has been saying "happy-day." It is the first thing often in the morning that she wakes up Mamma saying, and she sings it to her dollie through the day, and at night she will sit down in brother's little rocking chair, and rock away singing

---

[50] "Ode to a Baby" by Alice Muzzy.

..ppy-day, happy-day." She gets quite a tune to it sometimes, and Grandma thinks she is going to sing surely. She is a happy little girl, like her dear Papa, every day seems her best day.

Mama was gone down to New York City the first two weeks in April to attend to some business; she was expecting to come home on Saturday the 11th, but the Woman's Branch of the I. M. M. S.[51] wanted her to stay over to their Board Meeting Monday the 13th which she did; and that very day it so happened Edith was left all alone in the dining room a while. Grandma was in the house, but lying down. All the others were out. When Aunt Annie came in from feeding the chickens she found the baby Edith in the water-barrel in the milk room! This is a cask set in the floor, some 20 inches above the floor. There has always been some trouble to keep children from playing in it, but no one ever thought of their falling in. It is always full of water which runs in from the spring through a pipe. All think Edith must have fallen in head-first, there seems no other way she could have done it, but when Aunt Annie came in she was on her feet, paddling around, crying to get out. How such a little thing managed to get on her feet before choking and strangling in the water seems like a miracle, and that she never took any harm from the cold water seems another. She was shivering and pale when Grandma and Aunt Annie took off her wet clothes and put dry ones on, but she went to sleep soon after, and when Mama came home the next day she would never have known her darling had been in such danger if Grandma had not told her. How merciful it was of our dear Heavenly Father to spare dear baby's precious life. Mama is so thankful, and she prays that her baby may grow to be a wise, useful woman, and use the life God has given and preserved, to His glory.

"Grandma and the Baby!"

Grandma and the baby had their picture taken this month, like Grandpa and Sherwood did one year ago. We had thought it would be more trouble to make the baby keep still, but she was very good indeed, and both she and Grandma got a very nice picture. Almost everyone thinks Edith looks like her grandmother Sherwood.

---

[51] International Medical Missionary Society.

Journal of Edith Margaret Hall

Tuesday, August 18, 1896

    The Lord bless thee, and keep thee. Numbers vi. 24

    "She rules with subtle art and skill
        Excelling statesmen far,
    And 'neath her changeful humors still
        Her subjects loyal are;
    No heart rebels against her sway,
        Her actions meet no blame;
    In all her moods from grave to gay
        Her words attention claim."[52]

The last one you'd expect to spoil a child is Grandma Sherwood, yet Aunt Annie says she is surely spoiling Edith Margaret. Though she is naughty and Grandma knows she ought to punish her, she will say "oh she's so little—she don't know any better—it will be time enough when she's bigger." But often times Miss Edith does know better, and one day when she got up and stamped on some of Aunt Annie's flowers, that she had been well taught not to touch, Aunt Annie had to give her a good spanking, for Mamma was away, and Grandma said she "couldn't do it."

Little Miss Edith Margaret rules supreme over Grandma, and Joe and Dah, and she is beginning to know it Mamma fears. No matter much what she does, either dear Grandma or "old black Joe" is ready with an excuse for her. It is curious how much more Joe has always seemed to care for baby Edith than for her brother—it was just so much with Mamma when she was little and Uncle Walter—he seems to love girls best.

Edith Margaret weighs 28 pounds now, and is 33 inches tall standing. Circumference of the head is 18½ inches. Her cranium is not quite so large as Sherwood's at the same age, Mamma sees, but Dah, he says it's larger, and that she is going to have a larger head than Sherwood, but on referring to Sherwood's journal Mamma finds that brother's head measured 18½ inches when he was a 15 month old, while Edith is 19 months old today. Mama didn't record what brother's measured at 19 months, but at 17 months already it was 19 inches in circumference. However, Edith can talk more now than Sherwood did at 21 months, so the size of one's cranium doesn't always count in everything. She has added to her vocabulary pie, baby, bird, man, and see, and she says "see bird" and "see man" and "all dirty."

---

[52] "A Queen" from *Chambers Journal of Popular Literature, Science and Arts*, Edinburgh, 1895.

Mamma went home from Mount Lawn[53] at just about this time to see her dear babies, and Grandma let them sit up till nearly 9 o'clock to see Mamma when she came. She had been away from them four long weeks and she feared baby Edith might have forgotten her. But she had not, not one bit, she said "Mamma" as soon as she saw her and wanted to climb up in her lap at once, and then she clasped her dear little arms about Mamma's neck and gave her such a sweet hug. Nobody was quite like Mamma as long as she was there, yet she is very fond of Grandma and Dah, and rather looks to them when she gets hurt or gets in trouble anyway. She is a funny little midget and doesn't yet tell when she wants to go to the closet, though she can talk so much better than Sherwood when he began to tell—however, she is not quite old yet; but it does seem as if she could do better sometimes. The other day after soiling her diaper, she took a piece of paper and undertook to clean herself. Then discovering Grandma watching her she stopped and cried out, "Dah, all dirty" and waited for him to come and fix her up right again. Mamma hopes she may be easy to learn to be clean like brother was, but it just seems now as if she might not. Aunt Annie says, "Oh you'll have an awful time with her, you see." However, Sherwood was just about two years old before Mamma put drawers on him, and it does seem that Edith wear them surely by next January. We will see.

Joe took Grandma, Mamma, Dah, Sherwood and Edith out to Liberty for a nice ride the Saturday Mamma was home, and we made a little call at Uncle Frank's drugstore, and he gave the children some candy. They each got weighed also, and Sherwood has been gaining a little during the last four weeks, but weighs now only four pounds more than his little sister. However, as he is on the gain, and as Edith looks as fat and well as can be, Mamma thinks she better "let well enough alone" and not take them back with her to Nyack as she had it in her head to do when she came home. In only about three weeks now Mamma's work will be done at the C. H. C. H.[54] and then she hopes to have her darlings with her again all the time. The separation has been hard, but Mamma can't regret it, for her babies have been well taken care of, and besides Mamma has been able to look after over 2000 other children, medically, and she has enjoyed this work. Many an unfortunate little waif has received an outing who would not have "passed" if the C. H. C. H. had not changed physicians this year, and because Mamma lived at the Home, those who were sick could receive a better attention than ever before, as they have not had a doctor at the Home before.

---

[53] Rosetta was the physician in charge for the Christian Herald Fresh-Air Children's summer camp.
[54] Christian Herald Children's Home.

The Monday morning, Mamma left for her work again. Both Sherwood and Edith got up before 6 o'clock to see her off, and neither one cried, but they bravely kissed Mamma "goodbye" waving their little hands in parting.

Edith's lock of hair 2 years

The Sweetest lives are those to duty wed,
Whose deeds, both great and small,
Are close-knit strands of unbroken thread
Where love ennobles all.
The world may sound no trumpets, ring no bells;
The book of life the shining record tells.

The love shall chant its own beatitudes
After its own life working. A child's kiss
Set on thy sighing lips shall make thee glad;
A sick man helped by thee shall make thee strong;
Thou shalt be served thyself by every sense
Of service which thou renderest.   —Mrs. Elizabeth Barrett Browning

Sunday, October 18, 1896

Though Mamma started to write about her baby at this time, other duties interfered, and she never had a chance to write until after her little daughter had celebrated the second anniversary of her birthday, and then it was with difficulty and haste at odd intervals.

Monday, January 18, 1897

Thou crownest the year with Thy goodness. Psa. 65:11

"All day, upon my work intent,
    My busy feet pace to and fro,
And every energy is bent
    Upon each mission as I go:
And ever 'round my fingers twine
    These little hands that cling to mine.

'Wait Mamma,' cries a birdlike voice:
    'Don't leave me, let me go too'
Her loving eyes my heart rejoice;
    I linger, though I've much to do,

Journal of Edith Margaret Hall

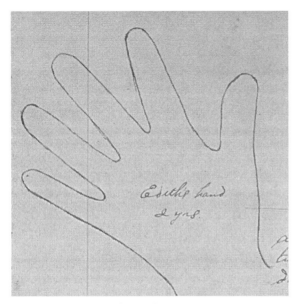

Edith's hand at 2 years

What would life be could I not find
This little hand that clings to mine?

Dear little hands! Oh, guide them, Lord
And keep them pure and clean;
So quick to do with loving might,
Turn them from all things mean.
To Thine own use I pray Thee, bind
These little hands that cling to mine."

January 18th has come around again, and this time finds Mamma's baby daughter two years old. How much she has gained in every way since one year ago, when Mamma wrote in the journal about her, one can only realize by comparing what she was then with now. Then she weighed 23 pounds, now 30, and she was 29½ inches tall, now 35½. Her head measured 18 inches in circumference, now it measures 19½ inches. And just see how her little hand has grown, and her "bonny brown hair." Then she wore 3½ shoes, now No. 6. Then she had but two little pearls in her mouth, now she has sixteen, and they are so white and even and pretty. Then she crept, now she walks and climbs, and jumps quite as well as brother, then she was just beginning to say a word or two, now she can talk almost as much as a brother. She attempts to say a great many things, and with fair success, has even begun to say "now I lay me" from having heard the brother say it. And she is in a hurry to add herself about God blessing "Mama, and Baba, and baby, and Annie, and Joe, for Jesus' sake, Amen."

Mamma is sorry that she has been too busy to keep much of an account of Edith's progress in language. Since Mamma took up work at Nyack last June, she has been able to write very little in her children's journals, and as Edith's vocabulary has been largely made up during this time, there is not as good a record of it as of Sherwood's. However, Edith began talking much younger, and has progressed much more rapidly than her brother did.

Grandma spent about six weeks with us here at 121 E. 45th Street. She brought Sherwood back the day before Thanksgiving. Edith was so glad to see them, and dear Grandma took a great deal of care of her little girl while she was here, and Edith was pretty happy; but since Grandma has gone what with not getting as good care, and with beginning to cut her second year molars, she is often unhappy now, and has such a forlorn expression to her face much of the time with the corners of her lips drawn down as though ready to cry. Mama is afraid she will grow that way if it continues much longer.

Well, this day, Edith Margaret's birthday, Mamma went out and bought a little frosted angel's food cake, and two little wax candles to put on it, and she lighted them, and put it before Edith at the dinner table, and she was very pleased with it. She quickly blew out one light, but kept the other sometime—but she is so fond of blowing out candles, she couldn't resist the temptation to blow it out too. Mamma lighted them for her a few times, and then she let her help cut the cake, and she had a nice time eating it. She gave brother and Mamma some, and thus ended the second anniversary of her birthday.

Edith 28 months old

How much we missed dear Grandma! How true the little poem at the beginning of this day is! How many times Edith's little clinging hand and "Mamma, me go" forces her to take her with her! As the help is not adequate for the work here at 121, Mamma has to take much more care of both Edith and Sherwood, than before, and they like it pretty well, and of course, soon learn not to want anyone else to help, and that makes it harder for Mamma. Edith takes a nap every day about 12 o'clock, when Grandma was here, she "byed her to sleep" but now Mamma does it. She has first a little lunch of warm milk and bread, and she soon shuts her little eyes, and can be laid down in the crib. At night she often asks to get into the crib without rocking or after being rocked just a little she will say "bedsh" and then Mamma puts her in, and she turns over and lies on her chest and stomach, generally pushing her head up to the very top of the crib and turning it a bit to one side. She almost never sleeps on her back, and always goes to sleep lying on her stomach. She often sleeps all night through, but sometimes, gets up to "Dee" as she always calls it. Sherwood says "shee."[55]

She calls water "audo", Sherwood says "auger." They both continue to call Yousanie "Dah," though Sherwood can say Yousanie plainly. They both call Grandma Baba yet too. Edith often strings words together just as grown-up people, such as "there, right there," "there, bŭbŭ's chair." She calls Sherwood bŭbŭ for brother, and has never called herself anything but "baby" yet. She says "Bubu come here," "blow my nose," "Mamma, see pretty flowers!" "Me no like," "no pinky me," she has always said "äm" for yes, but now she begins to say "esh." She calls cracker "kakar" and candy "nangie."

Here is Edith's picture taken four months later. Her hair is 5 or 6 inches long behind, and curls quite easily. Her front hair never grew long, only just now getting long enough to tieback. Mamma is going to have it all shingled soon. This picture makes baby Edith look older than she is, but it is pretty good of her, does not flatter her.

Friday, June 18, 1897

And a little child shall lead them. Isa. xi.6

"Perhaps there are tenderer, sweeter things,
    Somewhere in this sun-bright land,
But I thank the Lord for His blessings,
    And the clasp of a little hand."

Mama's baby is 2½ years old, and a big strong girl. She has been with Grandma Sherwood now ever since May 1st when Mamma happened to bring her up from New York just

---

[55] "Shee" means to "pee."

in time for her to help comfort dear Grandma and keep her from being so lonesome just when Aunt Annic was married and went away.

Grandma wrote to Mamma often. She said Edith was very happy and contented, "oh how she likes to go out in the orchard and pick flowers." Grandma wrote that she let Edith fuss around at night as long as she liked, when she would say, "I want to go to bed," and then she would turn her back around to Grandma to undress her. She always buttons and unbuttons her petticoat where it fastens to the waist in front then she says her little prayer, and goes right to sleep. She has not wet the bed or wet her drawers in the daytime once through the month. So Mamma's little daughter was pretty good with her dear Grandma.

Mamma and brother came home[56] the last of May, and now Edith is not quite so good a girl as when she was alone with Grandma. That seems to be always the way with children.

Edith seems to have grown stouter during the month, and having her hair cut also makes her look different—Mamma had Mr. Horn cut it the afternoon she left her with Grandma. She doesn't look so old as she did with it long. She has learned to talk quite a great deal more, she says "Gam-ma" now. She will say, "Rains, can't go out" or "Nice day, can go out." She likes to tease for candy—she will say, "Kangie, Kangie, peash gi me Kangie." One day she spied Mamma's paste bottle, and she asked, "What's in there?" Mama said, "Paste," then she asked, "Ain't paste good to eat?" and when told no, she said, "Berries good to eat." She had just been having her first strawberries, but they don't seem to agree with her or brother very well—Mamma never could eat them. She is quick enough to claim her things saying "that's mine." She says, "It hurts me so," and many other things—Mamma can't begin to keep track of her vocabulary now. One day Grandma, Mamma and the children took a walk down the lane, and Edith had evidently been there before with Mrs. Gordon (the woman that works here for Walter) as she ran on ahead, and said, "There is a nice lake over there." When we got near the brook, she also knew where to find some honeysuckles where Mamma used to have a little garden by her play-house when she was a little girl.

Today Edith had her first nosebleed. She fell giving it a sharp blow upon the stone furnace, and it bled profusely for a few moments. She was quite frightened.

Though Edith slept with Mamma the first night Mamma came home, most of the time she is quite content to sleep with "Gamma"—"my Gamma" she will say, "Let me take your arm" and she will hug it and go to sleep. Sometimes she will wake up in the night and say, "I can't see you, give me your face." She is quite an affectionate little piece. She will caress my face and say "nice mamma" or "my little mamma." She seems to think "little" is a term of endearment.

---

[56] The Sherwoods Farm in Liberty, NY.

Edith and her brother both take much interest in the packing for Korea which is almost done now. Every once in a while they will get in a big box or tub and say, "I am going to Korea, now."

"Edith's first letter to Mamma"

Monday, October 18, 1897, Lost!

We went to bed Sunday night on the good steamship *Empress of India* out upon the Pacific near the [blank] and when we awoke it was Tuesday morning, October 19—so the 18th was quite lost and Mamma couldn't write upon that date this time.

Saturday, October 23, 1897

I am the Lord, your Holy One, the creator of Israel, your King. Thus saith the Lord, which maketh a way in the sea, and a path in the mighty waters. Isa. 43:15, 16

> Sweet voyager on an unknown sea,
>   Thy tiny sails but just unfurled;
> Thy bark seems all too frail to be
>   Launched out where seething waters whirl.
>
> Though calm may seem the waves today,
>   The winds may lash them soon to foam;
> Then where will be thy fragile bark,
>   Fair, helpless thing so far from home?
> The little voyager smiles as sweet
>   As though no danger brooded o'er;

Unconscious of the storms 'she'll'[57] meet,
    'She'[58] sails serenely from the shore.

An unseen Pilot at the helm
    Looks smiling on the helpless child;
An angel, with a folded wing,
    Will guide the bark through waters wild.   —Emily Bugbee Johnson

There is so much to tell about what has occurred during the last four months of Edith's life, that Mamma will be obliged to leave unwritten for lack of time.

Soon after last writing, Uncle Charlie and family made a short visit at Grandma's home, and baby Julia[59] who was just beginning to sit alone was quite a treat for Edith. She wanted to hold her on her "loppie" as she calls her lap right away and she looked so sober and demure doing it. For weeks and months after, she often spoke of it saying "I held a baby on my loppie." Edith was also much interested in watching baby Julia nurse her dinner from her mamma's breast.

"Baby Julia"

The latter part of August, Yousanie, "my Dah," as Edith calls him, left Mamma's employ as he decided not to return to Korea with her. Edith missed him much, but as he only went down to Mrs. Adgate's house first, she saw him quite frequently and so didn't say so much about it. No doubt he misses baby Edith quite as much or more. He seems to love both her and Sherwood, dearly.

September 6th, Mama, Sherwood, and Edith left the dear old home-nest in Liberty, and turned their faces westward to the Far East. Good old Joe took us to the Depot—"Dah" went too, and Grandma went with us as far as Rockland feeling it would not be so hard to say "goodbye" this way, and that she would not miss Mamma and her babies so much afterward. She had a pleasant visit at Rockland, Beaverkill, Livingston, Mann and Parksville—was gone two weeks. Mamma, Sherwood and Edith went on to Utica where they had to stay all night with Margaret Jane Jones'[60] grandpa and grandma. The next noon on the way to the Depot they called at Mrs. Thorn's, sister of D. B. St. John Roosa[61]. That evening they arrived in Ogdensburgh

---

[57] Rosetta changed "he" to "she."
[58] Rosetta changed "he" to "she."
[59] Julia Sherwood is Rosetta's brother Charles Hurd Sherwood's daughter.
[60] Margaret Jane Jones ("Gretchen"), eldest daughter of Rev. George Heber Jones.
[61] Daniel Bennet St. John Roosa (1838 - 1908) was a well known ophtalmologist and otologist, the founder and president of the New York Post-Graduate Medical School. He was Rosetta's Professor when she was in training.

where Mamma's old college mate Dr. Mary Bryan[62] recently returned from India, was to meet them, and they spent a delightful two days' visit in her home. At a missionary meeting there the following day, Edith and Sherwood were dressed up in their Korean clothes, and later Dr. Bryan took some pictures of them, which are quite fair, and gives an idea how Edith looks when she feels a little strange or shy.

Sherwood and Edith after missionary meeting, Ogdensburgh

We went by boat *The Island Belle* to Brockville September 9th. Edith and Sherwood enjoyed the St. Lawrence[63] very much. Uncle Will Gray[64] met us, and we were soon once more at Aunt Alice's. Cousins Maud, Allan and Harry had grown very much—but not more than baby

---

[62] Dr. Mary Bryan took over Rosetta's work at New York Deaconess Home in 1890; she then served as a medical missionary to India.
[63] The Saint Lawrence River, which flows in a roughly north-easterly direction, connecting the Great Lakes with the Atlantic Ocean
[64] William Gray is William James Hall's sister Alice Hall's husband.

Journal of Edith Margaret Hall

Edith who the last time she was here was such a tiny child weighing only abou[t] taking only two tablespoonfuls of milk at a time for nourishment. Now she w[eighs] and eats good hearty meals, and holds her own with Sherwood or Harry eit[her]. only 3 weeks older than Sherwood, and before when we were here Sherwo[od] but now Harry is. He is a pretty good little boy and let baby Edith use his high chair all the time she was at Aunt Alice's.

Saturday, September 11th we went on to Glenn Buell to Grandpa Hall's. Grandma, Aunt Lillie[65] and all were very glad to welcome us. Everyone notices the most change in Edith, of course. We made nice visits at Aunt Jane Rowsom's[66], Uncle Boyd Hall's[67], Mr. Percival[68]'s, and Mr. Tourisse's and Mr. Gilroy's, and some calls at other places. Sherwood and Edith went in the old stone school house at Glenn Buell where Papa used to go to school, and which was his spiritual birthplace, also they saw the Athens High School which he attended later. Again they visited dear old Grandfather Bolton who is yet living, now confined to his bed with a broken and dislocated hip for these three years. He seemed quite as well as when last we saw him, engaged in conversation and even in singing quite heartily. Uncle William[69] just takes the best of care of him, devoting his whole time to him. Grandfather is an earnest hopeful Christian, and delights in Christian hymns and prayer. He is patiently biding the time when the Master shall take him home. He told Sherwood and Edith how when their Papa brought out those city children from New York to Charleston Lake, that he took him out there one day and introduced him to them, saying "Children, this is my Grandfather" and how they all bowed to him, and were so glad to see Dr. Hall's grandfather.

In a postal from dear Grandma written from Livingston Manor, she says, "How are my little children getting along? I suppose Grandma Hall takes my place now? How I would like to clasp them in my arms and give them a kiss once more—and I hope to sometime."

September 27th we left Brockville in the afternoon and went to Carlton Junction where we had to go to a hotel and wait till 2 o'clock in the morning to get our train for St. Paul. It made a very hard start—did not take a sleeper that night—but did the following—however, the children each got a whole seat upon which they could stretch out, and they slept pretty well. Reached St. Paul about 9 a.m. September 29th. Mrs. Jones[70] and her uncle met us at Depot; we spent the day with them. Margaret Jane Jones has grown quite a little, seems rather larger than Edith. She is much better behaved than when she visited us in New York. She obeys her mamma

---

[65] Lillie Hall is William James Hall's baby sister.
[66] Jane Bolton Rowsom is Grandma Hall's sister.
[67] Boyd Hall is Grandpa Hall's brother.
[68] Aunt Sarah Hall Percival's husband.
[69] William Bolton is the youngest brother of William James Hall's mother.
[70] Mrs. Margaret Bengel Jones.

Journal of Edith Margaret Hall

w rather better than Edith does, if anything. We spent a pleasant day in Mrs. Jones' uncle's home. Her father, Grandpa Bengel, was also visiting there, and 7 p.m. we started on for South Dakota—took a sleeper to Aberdeen, and reached Letcher, South Dakota about 10 a.m. September 30th. Brother was quite ill the most of the way, and was completely tired out when we reached Uncle David Powell's[71] so that Mamma had to put him to bed. Edith was pretty tired too, but after a good night's rest or rather a couple of them, both were quite themselves again, and they enjoyed their Dakota visit very much. Edith took great delight feeding some young chickens there, and rocking on the big straw stacks. Cousin Jason[72], who when a little boy like brother, used to live at Grandma Sherwood's house, and Mamma used to take a great deal of care of, is now a grownup young man twenty-four years old. He was so glad to see Sherwood and Edith, and he showed them books he used to have when a little boy at Grandpa's house, and cards that Mamma gave him then, also a little muslin scrap book she made for him of black and pink paper muslin pinked about the edge. Cousin Jason always took such good care of his things. I wish Mamma's children might do as well. Sherwood is quite careful, and Edith is learning to be more so.

Cousin Vira[73] just fell in love with Edith, said she was just her style of a little girl, so independent. She wanted very much to have Mamma leave her with them for the next five years and Uncle David and Auntie[74] would have liked it too, but Mamma couldn't think of sparing her darling so long as that. When Mamma was a little girl like Edith she used to sit upon Uncle David's lap and pull his whiskers, and Uncle David used to steal kisses just as he does now from baby Edith while she pulls his whiskers like Mamma used to. It all seems so strange to Mamma. It seems such a short time ago that she was in Edith's place, and now to think that Edith is her own girlie—she can hardly realize it. Mamma also has some little books that Uncle David gave her when she was a wee girlie, and some day she will give them to her children. Cousin Vira gave Edith a nice picture plate to eat from which says "Forget me not," and Auntie gave Sherwood one saying "Remember me." How well Mamma remembers when dear Grandma came home from Newburgh once when she was a little girl and brought her and Aunt Annie

---

[71] Rev. David M. Powell married Rosetta's half-sister Ada Elvira Sherwood then after Ada's death, to Adaline Annette Sherwood, also Rosetta's half-sister. Rosetta's father Rosevelt R. Sherwood lived 91 years and married three times. From the first marriage to Betsy Hurd, two children were born and Adaline Annette Sherwood is one of them; Betsy died of cancer at age 29. From the second marriage to Fanny Hurd, a distant cousin of Betsy, five children were born; Ada Elvira, William Fanton, Charles Hurd, and Frank Rosevelt are from this marriage. Fanny died of breast cancer at age 48. From third marriage to Phoebe Gildersleeve, Walter Hill, Rosetta, and Annie were born.

[72] Jason Gould Powell is son of Rev. David M. Powell and Adaline Annette Sherwood.

[73] Vira Powell, Jason Gould Powell's sister.

[74] Mrs. David M. Powell, née Adaline Annette Sherwood.

each a nice picture plate which they ate from till they were quite grown up. Mamma's had a picture of a little girl kneeling before a beehive watching the bees, and the two versus about

> "How doth the little busy bee
> Improve each shining hour."[75]

Our visit at Victor, South Dakota seemed only too short. It was so very pleasant and restful, but we had to leave Tuesday afternoon October 5th. Cousin Jason took us to the Depot at Letcher, a drive of ten miles over the prairies. Edith fell asleep. Cousin Jason gave the children a bag of candies, and we said "goodbye," and turned our faces toward St. Paul again arriving there Wednesday morning about 9 o'clock. Here at the Depot we were met by Dr. Harris[76] and Miss Pierce[77] who are new missionaries going out to reinforce W. F. M. S. work in Söul, and a little later Mrs. Jones and Gretchen came, and soon we were all off in a "tourist car" in the C. P. R.[78] We boarded ourselves all the way to Vancouver and Mamma's and the children's share was only $2.60 for 11 meals, and we lived pretty well too. There were only four other people in our car, so all had plenty of room and felt comfortable—and the children could play all they liked. Mama's babies don't get on very well with Gretchen—too near of an age—one seems as much to blame as the other. Mamma thought later when they got more used to each other they'd get on better, but there is little improvement. Each wants what the other has and neither wants to give up. Once in a while there is a temporary flash of generosity on the part of one or the other that is refreshing, but generally Mamma has to force Edith to give up or Mrs. Jones Gretchen according to circumstances. Sometimes Mrs. Jones would get the children all interested in some kindergarten songs or games or work which was very interesting, but Edith seems a little too young to care for it much yet, though Sherwood likes it. Gretchen's mamma has taught her quite a little kindergarten work, and she does nicely though nearly 2 months younger. Mamma has never tried to teach Edith anything of the kind though she feels she ought to soon, and must hay in some material for it before long.

We reached Vancouver 6 hours late—went to the Commercial Hotel. Edith was sick—had had for a day quite a touch of dysentery which continued during our stay at Vancouver. The first return she has had of the trouble since she was a little baby.

Monday, October 11th about noon we went on board the *Empress of India*. Our stateroom is 226 and is very comfortable. Edith sleeps with Mamma and Sherwood on the lounge,

---

[75] From Isaac Watts' poem, "How Doth the Little Busy Bee."
[76] Dr. Lillian N. Harris (1863 – 1902), sister of Mrs. E. Douglas Follwell, was a medical missionary to Korea 1897 – 1902. She died of typhus fever during her service in Korea.
[77] Miss Nellie Pierce came to Korea in 1897 for educational work and married Rev. Hugh Miller of Bible Societies in 1904.
[78] Canadian Pacific Railway.

though one night when it was very rolling, and Mamma had to have the side of her bed up, it was too narrow, and Edith slept in one end of brother's bed and made no fuss at all about it. The children had lunch and supper and went to bed all right before reaching Victoria. It was quiet sailing, but damp and cold, very foggy. We were on deck, but it was rather unpleasant.

Mama received several letters—one from dear Grandma. She says how much she would like to clasp her babies in her arms once more and give them a kiss, and she hopes to some day.

While in Canada Mama wrote Grandma about Edith talking naughty to Mamma and attempting to strike her sometimes, and refusing to obey promptly and this is what Grandma wrote about it. Mama read it to Edith, and she has been doing better since. Grandma says, "I am sorry you are having so much trouble with Edith. You must train her. Whip her hard and talk to her lots. You will have to be quite severe for she is stubborn. Take a whip and put it on her. Try to have her mind without threatening her if possible. I hope Sherwood will be a good boy and mind too. Try your best to bring them up right. It is business, every day at it, year in and year out."

Mamma and the children slept well and felt all right during the first afternoon and night on the sea, but by Tuesday morning there being considerable motion soon after awaking each were sick, and vomited at intervals of two or three hours all through the day. We did not try to dress, but kept in our berths. Ate and drank a little, the children slept a great deal. Wednesday morning we all felt better, and the children were not sick any more, but before Mamma could get them both dressed and herself, she vomited twice—that however, was the last of her sickness. Since then though we have had some pretty rough Sea and hard rolling with some pitching that has made others sick again, we have kept well, and have eaten every meal regularly. The children are very hungry for their meals and often tease for something between, though they eat about five times a day. Their meals are about one hour before Mamma's. Mamma goes with them and waits on them. There are about 15 children on board. All have nurses or governesses to attend to them except Mamma's and Mrs. Jones'.

Edith thinks it is pretty nice to call for most anything she wants to eat especially in the fruit line. If she doesn't have just what she wants she will say, "Mamma, ask the boy" for a banana, or pear, or orange or whatever is lacking. She has great faith that the "boy" can bring her anything she wants. She takes to it as naturally as if she were always used to it. The China boys like her, and she is not a bit afraid of them, though Gretchen is.

Sherwood and Edith are both so good to stay in the nursery or in Mamma's room or on deck when Mamma goes to meals, all she has to do is to promise to bring them something, and they have never gotten into trouble but once. Then Edith had a trouble, and somehow both she and Sherwood got to crying very hard so the Captain had to send the Stewardess to see what was the trouble.

At night they have their supper 5 o'clock then Mamma let's them play till 6:30 when the first gong for dinner sounds; then she puts them to bed. Sometimes they are asleep before 7:00, but if not Mamma leaves them then for dinner just the same. They say their prayers, and Mamma turns the electric lights off, and she always finds them fast asleep when she returns. They have never once made any trouble yet that way. Mamma always brings a few raisins or nuts or a nice piece of cake or something which they eagerly expect as soon as they awake, which is often about 5 a.m. and sometimes they don't get asleep again, and they never sleep later than 6 o'clock. At 6:30 the boy brings up some fruit and crackers, and then it takes from that time till 7:30 for Mamma to get them dressed and washed. Then 7:45 they [eat] breakfast—generally go up alone as Mamma is often not quite ready yet, though she gets up before they are through. The boy waits on them all right and they get on nicely. Mamma thinks they are both gaining in weight—they eat so much.

Monday, October 25th, we landed at Yokohama, and Edith had her first jinrikisha ride which she enjoyed after she got on Mamma's lap. She seemed a little timid at first when Mamma put her in with Sherwood alone.

Edith talks almost everything now, and says some very cute things sometimes or asks odd questions, but if Mamma doesn't put them down at the time she forgets them or at least can't recall them often when writing in her journal. She still calls candy "Kangie" and begs for it nearly every day.

Edith and Sherwood have attended both Sunday morning services on board ship and have been just as good as could be. They also as a rule behave well at the hour we missionaries spend together in Bible study and prayer.

We will have a week in Nagasaki, waiting for the *Higo Maru* to take us to Korea, and are due there on November 10th, Sherwood's birthday.

Empress of India passenger booklet, "Oct. 11-28, 1897"

Passenger List of the *Empress of India*, "October 11 - 28, 1897"

Edith's Catarrhal Pneumonia

Exposed October 6 – 9 to whooping cough on car from St. Paul to Vancouver. Had a slight attack of dysentery from 8th to 12th. Seasick all day 12th and did not eat. Stools undigested for a time but no more blood.

November 7 and 9—Seasick on Yellow Sea. Exposed to draft some on 9th. 8th and 9th and 10th bad coryza and some cough.

November 10—Landed at Chemulpo. Was pretty irritable all day. 7 p.m. went to bed—feel cold—a little later vomited her supper—was feverish and restless all night.

November 11—a.m. fever seemed lower. Had some nose-bleed. Is drowsy and don't care to eat. 11 a.m. T 103.4°, R 50, P 150. 2 p.m. T 101.8°, R 44, P 138. 5 p.m. T 102.4°, R 44, P 150. 9 p.m.

thermometer broke, R 38, P 140. Gave Castoria ʒ ii[79]. During past 24 hours gave Extract Aconite ♏i[80] in 8 or 10 divided doses. Fever seemed reduced in the evening, but China boy broke thermometer and could not tell for certain. Was restless and often startled through night. One cheek burning. Respiration rapid and rude.

November 12—7 a.m. R 38, pulse rapid. 9 a.m. R 38, P 144. Gave a little digitalis. Got a thermometer from Dr. Landis who also saw her. Coarse rales all over both lungs, wheezy breathing—fever seems gone. 11 a.m. T 100.4°. 1 p.m. T 100.8°, R 36, P 144. 4 p.m. T 102°, R 38, P 180. Gave a little more digitalis. She takes little or no nourishment, drinks a few sips of milk perhaps q.i.d. As Castoria has not acted, gave ʒ ii Syrup of Figs 8 p.m. 9 p.m. T 100.1°, R 36, P 120. Rales about the same, wheezy respiration. 3 a.m. A good stool, pulse very rapid and respiration 42. After the exertion, first part of stool constipated, last part fluid.

November 13—Drank a small cup of milk during the night. Asked for something to eat for the first this morning—wanted dry toast, but got her to eat toast soaked soft in milk. Has hard coughing spells but don't whoop. Lungs clearing up a little. 9 a.m. T 99.6°, R 36. Took a long nap after breakfast. Sleeps most of the time anyhow. 12 noon drank a cup cocoa, asked to write to "Gamma" and did so. 1 p.m. T 100.4°, R 36. 3 p.m. ate banana and cup of cocoa. 4 p.m. T 100.2°, R 32. Between 3 and 4 p.m. asked to sew and sat up in her little chair awhile. Seems to feel quite herself. 6 p.m. another banana and cup of cocoa and a little beef soup. 7 p.m. sleeping for the first this afternoon. 8 p.m. T 101°, R 32, P 120. Right lung clearing up, apex normal, middle lobe pronounced expiratory sound, base some rales. Slept well all night, little or no coughing. Wet herself about 1 o'clock, seemed to take a little more cold in the head. Drank a cup of milk.

November 14—Had a formed stool at 7 a.m. Drank a cup of milk and ate a banana. 8 a.m. milk, toast and cup of cocoa. Was washed, sat up some time playing with her blocks. 10 a.m. T 99.4°, R 36, P 126. Cross and irritable. 11 a.m. sleeping—Cheyne-Stokes respiration—during one minute there were only 14 respiratory movements in alternate groups of 3's and 4's each, with pauses of 6 seconds between. In another minute there were 24 respirations in groups of 2's and 3's. 2 p.m. has slept till now, asked for her blocks but doesn't want to eat. Temperature gone up to 101.5°, perhaps due to semisolid food? 4 p.m. T 102.8°, still does not want to eat. No doubt she ate solid food too soon—and probably also took a little more cold when she wet herself last night. Her nose runs badly again. Ate the juice of an orange and begged for banana and toast—and pancakes! 5 p.m. had a cup of cocoa, perspiring. T 102.5°, R 40, P 132. Sleeping again. 6 p.m. ʒ i Syrup of Figs. 6:30 p.m.

---

[79] 2 drams, about 0.25 ounce.
[80] 1 minim is about 1 drop.

ate quite a little soup. Still perspiring some. 9 p.m. T 101.1°, R 40, P 120. Sleeping, but got her up to urinate. 11 p.m. good stool.

November 15—7 a.m. stool with some mucus, complained of some tenesmus. 9 a.m. T 99.6°, R 38. Drank a cup of milk during night—and had hot cup cocoa for breakfast. Washed her dollie and wrote a letter to "Gamma and Dah" and lay down to rest 10 a.m. Had 2 stools undigested milk, some mucus and tenesmus. A short nap between 10:30 and 11:30. 12 noon a cup of cocoa, teased for toast. 1 p.m. T 101°, R 38, P 126. Nose some better today. Slept between 1:30 and 3 p.m. and went off again after taking temperature, had a little drink of milk. 3 p.m. T 102°. 5 p.m. slept and awoke in perspiration, T 101.6°. 6 p.m. ate some beef soup. 9 p.m. ate some beef soup, T 99.8°

November 16—8 a.m. T 98°. 8:30 a.m. cup of cocoa and chewed a little beef steak. Moved to a little room. 10 a.m. had her first sponge bath under cover and change of clothes. 11 a.m. T 99.2°, got doses of Spts. Ammonia Aromat. at 10 and at 11 a.m. She went quietly to sleep then after her sponging of and change of clothes—and her respiration was 33 and pulse 108 at about 12 noon the lowest pulse she has had. 1 p.m. awoke, had cup of cocoa but refused some nice canned peach. T 100.5°—went off to sleep again. 3 p.m. T 102°, perspiring freely, ate cup of cocoa. 3:30 p.m. Calomel gr 1/10 and food. 2:30 p.m. Mrs. Jones and Gretchen came and staid till about 4 p.m. Edith awoke in perspiration, didn't get time to take temperature till. Had cup cocoa. 5:30 p.m. T 99.5°. Had juice of 2 oranges. 6 p.m. large cup chicken soup with rice. 7:30 p.m. Calomel gr 1/10 and soda again. Spts. Ammonia Aromat. continued this day about ℳxx taken. 9 p.m. slept well.

Wednesday, November 17—7 a.m. formed stool. Sucked an orange. 9 a.m. ate a little milk, toast and half cup cocoa. Semisolid stool, phlegm in both stools. 10:30 p.m. T 99.2° after sitting up to be washed and have bed made. Drank orangeade and went to sleep. 12:30 p.m. awoke, T 102.4°. Had cup chicken soup. Drowsy and breathing oppressed. Slept till 2:30 awoke perspiring and feeling brighter. Gave her Spts. Am.[81] And a little later gr ½ quinine sulphate pill to swallow with some orangeade, but she chewed it, and soon vomited. Later drank cocoa 1 cup. Still perspiring but bright and playful—will sit up to write and cut papers. Always urinates 2 or 3 times freely while perspiring. 6 p.m. ate big cup beef soup. Sat up 1 hour wrapped up by stove playing quite as herself. 8:30 p.m. T 98.5°, P 120. Body still moist, perspiring more and long today than before.

November 18—Body and hands kept moist all night. Slept well, little cough. Bad dreams toward morning. 5 a.m. sleeping, R 24. 7 a.m. T 97.5°, R 28, P 120. Ate an orange. 9 a.m. breakfast of rice and milk and cocoa. 10 a.m. T 98.1°. Dr. Landis called again. Is unable to decide whether baby has whooping cough at all or not. Thinks she has had catarrhal pneumonia—unable to decide yet, if

---

[81] Aromatic Spirits of Ammonia.

temperature now is due to that alone or to malaria. 11:30 a.m. T 97.6°, R 28, P 116. Is not at all sleepy yet. 12 noon ate an orange quite soon after some cold cocoa while gone to lunch she vomited mostly orange. 12:30 p.m. had promised her fish and rice as she had no fever but after the vomiting tried to put her off with milk, but she wanted the rice and fish so much gave it to her and she made quite a nice dinner drinking some milk too. She would say "nice rice," "nice fish," and enjoyed it so much. 1 p.m. had just now gone off to sleep for the first today. Slept till 4 p.m.—when temperature was 99.2°. As her respiration was only 28-36 and pulse 112-118 while sleeping, doubt if she had any use of temperature.

6 p.m. T 98.5°. Sat up in big chair by fire until 8 p.m. Ate beef soup and a little piece of bread and butter for her supper. Certainly seems quite well—as busy as she can be cutting paper, writing, playing with her dolly or blocks. Didn't go to sleep till 9:30 p.m. Slept well. No coughing to speak of. Awoke once and had her Spts. Am Aromat. which she used about ℳxL during the 24 hours.

November 19—8 a.m. had orangeade and abdominal massages but no stool during forenoon. None since the 17th. 9 a.m. breakfast of rice and milk and cup cocoa. Was washed and wrapped up in blanket in big chair and sat by stove until 1 p.m. Then put her in bed, she teased for an orange, which often eating she went to sleep about. 1:30 p.m. her dinner was rice with butter and sugar. 2:30 coughing spell. 3:30 coughing a little. 4:30 p.m. awoke T 98.1° Drank cup of cold cocoa after taking her medicine.

Saturday, November 20—Edith got up 7 a.m. and had breakfast in the dining room for the first—was bundled up good and "steward" carried her to hatoba, and we went up on the River boat to the Söul landing. Edith sat in her little chair in the ladies' cabin and played with her dolly or blocks quietly most all the time. Mrs. [blank], wife of the commander of the American Gun boat at Chemulpo and Mrs. Jolly wife of British Consul at Chemulpo both thought she was a remarkable good child and she certainly has been wonderfully good all through this sickness and convalescence. Much better than when she is well. She is so content and happy and amuses herself so well. She coughed but once going up the river. We started about 10 a.m. and landed about 4:30 p.m. It got quite dark before we reached the W. F. M. S. Home. Mamma carried her on her lap in a chair, and she was as warm and nice as possible—and was none the worse for the trip. We passed through rows of silk gauze lanterns in front of the Palace, ready for the Imperial funeral of the Queen on the morrow.

November 24—Thanksgiving Day. Edith has improved right along, has scarcely coughed once, and is quite well. Sherwood does not cough either and it seems scarcely probable now that either had the whooping cough. Edith's attack must have been catarrhal pneumonia, pure and simple—not as a complication. She has made a perfect recovery apparently. We took chairs and rode down to Papa's grave today. It is just 3 years ago November 24th that his body was placed there.

January 18, 1898

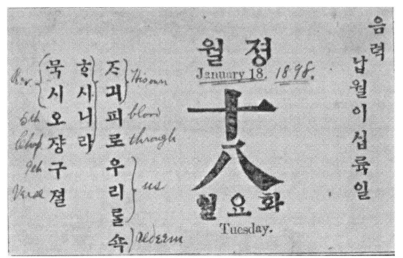

"음력 납월이십륙일, 정월 十八 화요일, Tuesday, January 18, 1898. ᄌ긔피로우리롤속ᄒ시니라 묵시오쟝구절"[82]

> And I smiled to think God's sweetness
>   Flows around our incompleteness, —
> 'Round our restlessness, His rest.   —E. B. Browning

Today Mamma's baby daughter celebrates her first birthday in Korea, ten-thousand miles away from the land of her birth. She is three years old today, and Mamma invited three little guests at 3 o'clock to come and play, and have "choke-dogs[83]," nuts, and hot maple sugar with her and Sherwood. These were Noland Miller, Mary Appenzeller, and Madeline Hulbert, and they all enjoyed themselves pretty good, played nicely, and no accidents occurred. There was a light snowfall, but not enough snow to drop the "choke-dogs" on, so Mamma dropped them in cold water. They seemed to be something new for them all. The nuts we had were filberts and almonds that Aunt Jane[84] bought for the children just as we were leaving Brockville.

---

[82] "Lunar calendar December 26, Tuesday, January 18, 1898. Have redeemed us to God by your blood. Revelation 5:9."
[83] Cheese, especially hard cheese. Origin: Isle of Wight cheese, nicknamed "choke-dog" and "Isle of Wight Rock." In later 19th century, as Island farmers concentrated on the production of cream and butter, only skimmed milk was left to make cheese out of, and so it soon became dry and hard.
[84] Mrs. Jane Bolton Rowsom, William James Hall's maternal aunt.

They had half of them at Christmas, and the remainder now. The maple sugar Mamma bought at Uncle Fanton's[85] store in Liberty. Edith got a very nice large doll with brown eyes and flaxen curls from Gretchen Jones, and Mamma gave her a cunning little set of table, four chairs, and a lounge in bamboo work for her dolly, and a silver dollar from Grandma. She was delighted with her presents. She says she will call her doll "Mary" because it has hair like Mary Appenzeller, and brother wanted to call it Mary. An accident happened to Mary Doll, however, before noon, which prevented her appearing at the children's party in the afternoon. Edith had her tied on to her back Korean fashion, and somehow she slipped to the floor cracking her skull. Edith almost cried, but remembering Mamma had repaired such troubles before now she came in and asked her to "paste" it and Mamma told her she must go and ask Miss Rothweiler for the glue which she did, and Mamma fixed it, and tied a tape around it tightly and put it away on the shelf to dry. It is the finest doll Edith has yet possessed firsthand. It has a bisque head, kid body, nice underclothes, a pretty white dress, red sock, red hat with white quills, black stockings, and what pleases Edith most of all is, little slippers with buckles. It is the first doll she has had with slippers that she could take off and put on. Sherwood tried to persuade her that "Mammas study and Papas take care of the babies" but he had to be put off with sitting down in his rocker beside the mamma and her dolly Mary, and reading the newspaper to them while dollie was rocked to sleep.

It was a long happy day for the three-year-old. She says "three ores"—playing with her new dollie till most dinnertime, then after dinner Mamma hurried to give her her nap so Mamma could go early to the hospital, and get back in time to treat the children. It has gotten to be the custom when Sherwood and Edith go to sleep well for their nap, for Mamma to leave an envelope by them to find when they awake with some candy, or cake or maple sugar or nuts, or some little treat, so this time Mamma left the little set of chairs etc. in a box, and Mamma would liked to have seen Edith's face when she awoke and took them out one by one; but Mamma had more patients than usual at the hospital and didn't get up until after she had awakened for some time. Then very soon the wee guests came, and everything was merry until it was time for them to go home, then she and Sherwood accompanied them home, and returned for their supper, which was a half hour later than usual, and they ate very much, more than usual, so that they were still eating at 6 o'clock when the ladies have their supper. Sherwood and Edith have a little round table in one corner of the dining room, all to themselves, using the little chairs Mamma bought them in Japan. The Amah waits on them. Mamma fears it would be better for their manners if they sat up in high-chairs at table with the ladies, but there doesn't seem to be room. This way, they are getting to be often rude and noisy, getting up from their chairs and running around now and then between courses, and Mamma dislikes to punish them there and have them cry before all the ladies, and her room is so far away (away out of doors)

---

[85] Dr. William Fanton Sherwood, Rosetta's brother.

that it is not convenient to send them to their room when they need punishment, and so they go without too often. But Mamma thinks it will be better when they can sit down to the table with other folks again. They will probably eat better too. Edith has been eating very poorly of late, but sometimes if Mamma takes her on her lap and feeds her, she will eat well of the very things she will not even taste of at her little table. Mama is giving her a little quinine for her appetite. She takes it pretty well in Syrup of Yerba-Santa. Since her sickness at Chemulpo, she has been pretty well save for one severe attack of left earache with considerable fever (103°), was in bed a day and a half with it—suffered considerable the first 12 hours. Put warm cocaine solution in and later gave it a bit aural douche which seemed to help most. This was before she had had quinine, as Mamma was unable to get any in a shape she could take until she got almost well at Chemulpo. Since the ear trouble she has complained but once a little of it again, but has complained several times of a feeling cold along about 4 o'clock in the afternoon, and that together with her lack of appetite seemed to call for the quinine.

During her illness at Chemulpo, all of her own accord, she began calling Mamma "Ma," and never once said Mamma again for over two weeks. Now, she seldom says Ma. She seems quite persistent— for instance she would ask Mamma to bring her a certain towel, and Mamma would put her off one way and another, but finally said she would get it for her when she get up, so then she plans for an excuse to get Mamma up, it works, and a little later she says, "Now, Ma, give me the little baby towel." She will cut paper a half hour at a stretch, uses her thumb and forefinger. She will cut spirals—at last cuts everything into very tiny bits, is careful to keep all in her box. She often asked to see the picture of herself in the case of Mamma's watch when her pulse was counted—she calls it "Gamma's baby." Sometimes she will sing to herself, "My Gamma, my Dah, my Joe." One night, shortly before Christmas, she was really homesick for her Grandma, and cried and fretted and wouldn't be comforted. Dr. Harris came in, and kindly helped to get her out of it, by telling her nice stories. Sometimes she says that she dreams about "Gamma" and when asked what "Gamma" was doing she replies "sewing"—sometimes it is "Joe" and he is always "going to Liberty."

Edith says "O, pshaw" which sounds very cunning from her, but Mamma is sorry she has learned to use it. She has gotten it from both Mamma and Grandma, I fear. Sometimes when Mamma doesn't reply to her right away she will say, "You don't seem to talk to me." She doesn't use a very good grammar sometimes but will ask, "Didn't you ain't got anymore?" She says, "I want <u>ax</u> for anymore now," "Amah don't ax the boy for any water." She and Sherwood both call putting their clothes on as well as taking them off "undress."

One day she gave Sherwood her sack to put on while she put on his overcoat, and she said, "Sherwood you be a girl, and I be a bŭ-bŭ[86]." Edith called Christmas "Kiphens day." It was the first time she has heard about Santa Claus or a Christmas tree. She went to an entertainment at the Söul Union where all the children were invited to a Christmas pie, and they had Santa Claus there. She got a nice little doll. Later all were invited to a Christmas tree at Holly Underwood's. Here she got a cunning little set of dishes and she was delighted. She used these now to set a little table with that she got today. However, as she and brother had both been rather naughty in spite of the fact that people told them if they were not good old Sana wouldn't put anything in their stockings when they hung them up Christmas Eve, when they awoke Christmas morning they really didn't find anything. It didn't make as much of an impression on Edith though as upon Sherwood, for she did not remember last Christmas. He felt pretty bad, and when he told the ladies over in the dining room, they told them because they felt sorry for him that old Santa Claus didn't give them anything, they would give them something. So they each got a couple of balls, and Edith a picture book and Sherwood a pretty puzzle, and both had candy and nuts. Mamma told them if they'd try and be good a whole week she would let them hang up their stockings New Year's Eve, and send old Santa Claus now. So they really try to do a little better, and got a little Japanese house filled with nice homemade candy (made by Mrs. Jones), nuts, oranges, and a doll. That night Edith prayed for a "big clean doll" and in the morning she found hung to the same nail with her stocking a large rag-doll, with the long white baby clothes freshly laundried that had been on, the baby Cousin Maud gave her in Canada. It went right to her heart. She plays with this dolly mostly, for Mamma will only let her have her new birthday doll once in a while.

Quotations from Grandma's letters:

"How is my little Tot getting along? Has she given up taking naughty talk? I do hope she is a better girl and how is the little man Sherwood? I think you will have more trouble to train Tot than you will him. Did they talk of us when they were on the water, and what did they say when they got out of sight of land? Were you all seasick at once or more than once? Tell us all the particulars. Now, I will close—can't write to the children this time. Thank Tot for the one she sent. Tell Sherwood to write too. God bless us all, keep us safe, and let us meet again. Mother"

---

[86] "brother" in her baby talk.

Journal of Edith Margaret Hall

Poor Grandma, her last letter brought word she had broken her arm. She was at Uncle Fanton's for sometime first, and then went down to Uncle Walter's, which she and Joe both are likely to spend the winter now. She writes from there.

"Oh, dear child, little Sherwood and Edith, how do I miss you! When I get over this lameness I will bring your pictures here and hang them up in this room. Now when I want to see you, I open the book, and there I see you and your dear Papa too."

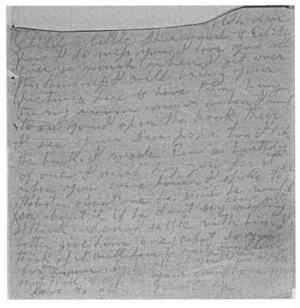
Grandma's letter

Grandma's picture with Edith on her lap is right up near where Edith gets dressed every morning, and she often gives her a good morning kiss. Tonight she wanted to get up and kiss the picture after she had gotten into bed, but Mamma carried it for her instead.

Edith begins to talk a little Korean, though so far, she doesn't seem to try to pick it up as much as Sherwood. All she really uses is 조심호오 for "be careful," and 어셔어셔 for "hurry hurry!" They have quite a good Amah—a young widow, a Christian baptized, "Nettie." She is industrious and a very good worker for a Korean, but she has not a very good knack for getting on smoothly with the children. She prefers to sit and sew to looking after them, and though Mamma tries to study faithfully every morning for three hours, it is often disturbed in looking after the children in one way or the other. Sometimes, Mamma wishes she had another room to study in, but it is probably better not—for no doubt a proper oversight over her babies is quite as much or more her duty than studying Korean, especially just now when they are so young, and among a strange people. How often Mamma, as well as they, has wished that Grandma might be here with us. It would be just lovely, if it were not for the terrible journey of getting here.

Edith says, "Now I lay me" all alone now. She prays, "God bless all those Korean children," and for our W. F. M. S. ladies here she says, "God bless all them ladies" though sometimes she says their names separately. She kneels by the bed now, just before she gets in, and has not for a long time not wanted to pray.

Journal of Edith Margaret Hall

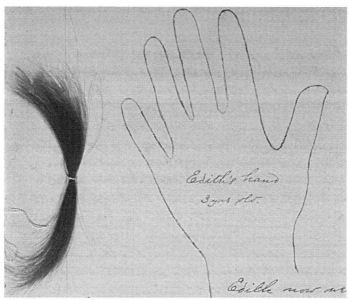

"Edith's hand 3 years old"

Edith now weighs 34½ pounds, having gained 2½ pounds since she left America, 4½ pounds during the year, she is 39 inches high having gained 3½ inches since her last birthday—her head measures only ¼ inch more, that is 19¾ inches in circumference. Her last birthday, she wore No. 6 shoes, and now she wears No. 8½. Edith's head measures exactly the same, and she is the same weight that her brother was when he was three years old, but she 1¾ inches taller. She too for some time back has not eaten well, nothing like as much as she used to, doesn't care for potatoes and bread as she did. She complains often of feeling cold about 4 p.m. and Mamma has been giving her a little quinine in Syrup Yerba-Santa. She doesn't like it, but takes it fairly well. She takes a nap every afternoon from 1:30 or 2 p.m. to 3 or 3:30 p.m., and brother does too now, and they go to bed at 7:30 p.m. getting up about 6:30 a.m. They go to bed pretty good generally, and often get dressed and washed without any trouble, but sometimes quarrel as to who shall be washed or dressed first, each wanting it to be the other. Mamma has to spank Edith quite often. She got in the habit of saying "naughty mamma" and Mamma didn't take much notice of it at first, but later she found she had to punish her to make her stop it. But as a rule Edith is pretty good to mind—she is affectionate and likes also to hug and say "good mamma." Mamma thinks she begins to look like the early pictures of Mamma, but some think she looks more like Papa than Sherwood does. When alone she plays nicely and can amuse herself well, better than her brother, but with others she is apt to get into more or less trouble. She seems to have quite a bump of order which is developing fast, and she generally keeps her play things in place, picking them up and putting them away before leaving the room; and she always picks her clothes up from the floor when undressing, and puts them in order on a chair, sometimes neatly folding each. She has also begun to straighten up Mamma's tray on the writing desk, putting pens, pencils, ruler, paper cutter, glue, paste, ink., etc. where Mamma likes them—and also the little trays for pins etc. on the bureau she loves to arrange. Of course she gets into mischief sometimes when no one is watching her and she comes across some of Mamma's medicine tablets or pills, she samples them, sometimes spills them, and doesn't always get them back where they came from, but Mamma imagines that many little three-year-olds would get into more trouble than Edith if their mammas had so much medicine within reach of their busy little fingers. She never spills Mamma's ink bottle anymore, and is daily improving in many things.

> "I love the coming woman,
>   I love her pretty ways,
> With music and with sweetness
>   She fills my fleeting days;
> I kiss her laughing dimples,
>   And stroke her hair of gold,
> For my dainty coming woman
>   Is only 'three'[87] years old."

Edith's Rubeola[88]

Exposed at Korean house January 28, 1898.

Saturday, February 5—Spoke of feeling sick before she got up. Ate nothing but a part of an orange for breakfast, and vomited about 8 a.m. Gave Syrup of Figs ℨ ii 9 a.m. Slept some and vomited again 10 a.m. Respiration 26. No stool today, but had one yesterday. Slept the most of the day and ate nothing—drank a little—urinated 3 times during the day. At 5 p.m. gave grade ℨ ii Syrup of Figs. 9 p.m. awoke and wanted to vomit but didn't—doesn't complain of pain.

Temperature 6 p.m. 103.8° (axilla)
                     9 p.m. 102.8°, pulse 118, respiration 32

Saturday, February 6—
6:30 a.m.	Had a little Aconite and Bryonia
7 a.m.	Temperature 100°—Santonin & Calomel āā[89] gr ½. Syrup of Figs.
7:30 a.m.	Had good stool.

---

[87] Rosetta changed "four" to "three" from the original poem, "A Woman of the Future," to match Edith's age.
[88] Measles.
[89] āā means "of each."

Journal of Edith Margaret Hall

10:30 a.m.	Temperature 98.6° P 132 R 20. Ate a cracker and orange and some cocoa for breakfast. Sleeping till 12:30.
12:30 p.m.	Temperature 99.6°, pulse 138. Wants some orange.
1 p.m.	Ate crackers and milk and juice of 2 oranges. Had liquid stool containing bile—no signs of worms.

Sunday, February 7—
7 a.m.   Temperature 98.8°. Seems quite well today.

Monday, February 8—Alright this morning. Went to sleep as usual after dinner. Amah was sick and when Mamma went to hospital left word for her and brother to go out in the jinrikisha when they awoke. It is a sunshining day, but rather cold.

Edith did not get well-wrapped, and when she came home complained much of the cold, but seemed alright later, but sleepy.

Tuesday, February 9—Slept till 7:30 then came over to breakfast. Didn't eat much. Eyes suffused and nose running, rather dumpish. Played with doll, but went nearly asleep rocking it and then wanted to be rocked herself. Went to sleep about 11 a.m. and slept till 12:30 when Amah wrapped blanket around her and brought her to the dining room. Miss Rothweiler fed her a little rice and milk. Her face looked as if the rash was coming out. She slept nearly all afternoon. Ate a little soup and some crackers for supper. Gave her ʒ iß of Syrup of Figs. She has had ℳ ii-iii doses of Spts. Ammonia Aromat'icus about every one hour through the day. Coughs quite a little, began Sunday p.m., but much more today.

8 p.m.	Temperature 103.2°, pulse 160, respiration 32.
8:30 p.m.	Vomited a little. Very faint rash on body.

Wednesdays, February 10—Broken out well this morning.
8 a.m.	Good stool, ate toast and cocoa.
9 a.m.	Temperature 99.8°, pulse 132, respiration 26

Thursday, February 11—Face almost rough, but beginning to fade from forehead. Gave Syrup of Figs again as had no stool today.

Friday, February 12—Two good stools, rash fading. Has a few spells now and then of that hard iron cough. Continued Aromatic Spirits of Ammonia as cough increased.

Saturday, February 13—Practically well. Gave sponge bath and change of clothes. Has good appetite. Will allow to go out in sunshine tomorrow.

Journal of Edith Margaret Hall

Edith's Dysentery

Left Söul April 29, 1898. Sailed on the *Hai Riong* April 30th, 3 p.m.

Saturday, May 1—Some diarrhea. Gave a dose of Castor oil and Rhubarb and noon. Had 2 or 3 good movements before bedtime.

Monday, May 2—No more movements and didn't urinate from 2 p.m. till 8 p.m. when we arrived at Pyong Yang.

May 3, 4, 5—Seemed fairly well.

Thursday, May 5—Wanted to go to bed early, but didn't go to sleep before 2 a.m. Had a throat cough, vomited several times; had eaten ice cream that afternoon. Restless complained of abdominal pain. Towards morning, had her drink cup of warm salt water but she didn't vomit it. Thought it would act as a saline cathartic and let it go. Kept her in bed that day. Had diarrhea only. Seemed better. Had only 2 stools. Countenance looked bad—fretful and no appetite. Kept in bed all day, though she seemed brighter. Has had only semisolid food the last 3 days, but yesterday swallowed some hard kernels of corn partly chewed, when saw a little of this in morning stool washed her out with a little saltwater and disinfections. Afternoon showed some symptoms of dysentery, pain and tenesmus and sitting long at stool. Put on liquid diet. Had a fair night. Since the 6th, gave Bismuch gr i + Ipecac gr 1/60 + Calomel gr 1/40 t.i.d.[90] and after stools.

Monday, May 9—Had some 6 stools during day. All containing blood, and what looked like chopped bloody bowel. Very little food or mucus. Had 3 enemas of tannic acid, retained one small one in the afternoon about 15 minutes, but others at once ejected. And none apparently did any good. Bismuth and Calomel, and Ipecac tablets finished this morning and gave Salol gr i t.i.d. Takes very little food. During night after tannic acid injection at 9 p.m. till 4 a.m. had 10 stools, of same nature—bloody tissue. Was restless and in pain. Much tenesmus. Bedpan. Took a little Mellin's Food once. Had to give Chloroanodyne for her to get any rest at all. During 24 hours, took about 12 ℳ. 3:30 a.m. gave 3 ounces of tannic acid injection. Had 3 stools in next half hour. Gave 2½ ℳ Chloroanodyne and Salol gr i, and little cracker in chicken broth, she got to sleep 4 a.m.

Tuesday, May 10—Slept well until about 6:30. Ate a half cup of cocoa with Nestles Food for breakfast. Had another wash followed by 3 stools. While sleeping injected 3 ounces of tannic acid solution, but she awoke shortly and wasted stool—had 3 more. Gave then a dose of Bismuth and Spts. Frumenti ʒ ß. Had had Chloroanodyne sometime before when she complained so bitterly of stomachache. Was sleeping 10 a.m. Slept till 12 noon. Had 6 stools mostly in napkins, bit 12 noon and 3 p.m. Took a little cocoa. Had Bismuth and Chloroanodyne and whiskey. Will stop tannic acid

---

[90] Three times a day.

Journal of Edith Margaret Hall

3 p.m. Rice starch Bismuth and Opii Camph injection retained it perhaps 15 minutes then 3 actions before 4:30 p.m.

4:30 p.m.	Again sleepy, but had 5 or 6 motions before 6:30 p.m. Urinated at one of them forced down a little bit of milk with Mellin's Food and a little gelatin. Complains bitterly of stomachache after eating. Gave Chloroanodyne, Spts. Frumenti and Bismuth again.
6:30 p.m.	Sleeping.
7:30 p.m.	Took a little chicken broth after Bismuth. 2 stools before 8 o'clock.
8 p.m.	Consultation with doctors Wells and Follwell. Treatment to be Dover's powder gr ii every 3 hours. A high washout in the morning, and rice starch injections with Bismuth continued. Before 10 p.m., 2 stools.
10 p.m.	Dover's powder, Valentine's beef juice ʒ ß[91]
11 p.m.	Motion

Wednesday, May 11—

12 midnight	Motion
12:30	Motion
1 a.m.	Motion
1:30 a.m.	Motion. Gave Dover's powder and milk with Mellin's Food 1 a.m.
2 a.m.	Another motion. Gave injection of rice starch and Bismuth, which she retained till 4 a.m. then had 2 motions and no more till 6 a.m. Urinated. Gave Dover's powder at 4 a.m. and beef juice.
7 a.m.	Dover's powder and milk and Mellin's Food. Promptly ejected the whole. Waited a little time, gave Bismuth in starch followed by a little beef juice and 7:30 repeated the Dover's powder, asked for water for the first since 9th.
10 a.m.	Washed out intestines using one catheter inserted the half length and a return catheter about 3 inches and 2 inches. Just before doing this she had the largest bloody stool she has had containing more fluid. Used 2 pints water with ʒ ii sodium chloride. Only the very first of return flow was slightly tinged with blood. The rest was clear. When about half done she begged so to have motion, withdrawal catheters. She passed only clear water. Reinserted and finished. Within 5 minutes, had motion with much tenesmus, passed some bloody fluid and black pollywog looking stuff. Had more motions in short succession, much tenesmus, so gave starch and Bismuth injections again which she retained only 50 minutes. Had 2 or 3 motions by 11:30 a.m. Gave Dover's and beef juice. Slept lightly on bedpan. Doesn't like at all to have it removed.
12 noon	Wanted to vomit, but ended with stool.
1:30 p.m.	Urinated. 2 motions. Drank a small cup cocoa.
2 p.m.	Dover's and some cow milk ʒ ß[92]. Wanted another, but got her off to sleep.

---

[91] ½ fluid dram = 30 minims or about 30 drops. ß or ss means half.
[92] Half ounce. ʒ is a sign for fluid ounce.

3:30 p.m.	Large bloody stool again. Drs. Wells and Follwell came. Gave another salt water high washout with like result of morning.
5 p.m.	Gave Dover's powder in water, and one spoonful of beef juice mixture, when she ejected the whole together with cup of cocoa and milk. Had to change her clothes. Tr. Opii[93] ♏iv by rectum.
5:15 p.m.	Bismuth in "meme"[94] by mouth.
5:45 p.m.	Beef juice. Had 2 passages.
6:30 p.m.	Tried to give some hard Horlicks milk but she wouldn't try it. Asked for water about 7 p.m. Vomited beef juice and water. Had more passages. Urinated. Complained of pain more bitterly than ever over umbilicus. Passages look again more like they did yesterday, as if a new portion were breaking down. Refuses to take anything as yet. In desperation offered her some Chloroanodyne again which she took about 4 ♏ of.
7:45 p.m.	Dropped off to sleep on bedpan—can't bear to have it removed.
8:30 p.m.	Tr. Opii ♏iv in "meme" per rectum while sleeping. Retained till 9:45 p.m. A small passage.
10 p.m.	Absolutely refuses, ice, milk or anything in mouth, took a little ice water. Seems more herself, but very fretful.
10:30 p.m.	Chloroanodyne ♏iiß[95] and took a very little meat juice. Temperature 100.1°.
10:45 p.m.	Vomited all again. Passages small. Feel like never urging her to take anything again, for each time have insisted upon it, she has vomited all. Absolutely refuses even ice or water.
11 p.m.	Another Tr. Opii, Bismuch, "meme" injection—Got all ready and she had another small stool, so deferred till 11:30 p.m.
11:30 p.m.	Gave it while she was sleeping, and all seemed well until 12 midnight when she vomited with retching, followed by stool. At last got her to take a bit of cold water with Spts. Frumenti ♏x. Will not get off of bedpan.

Thursday, May 12—

12:30 a.m.	Prepared a hypoderm. of morphine gr 1/20 should she be restless and unable to take anything by mouth or rectum. But is resting now.
1:30 a.m.	Stool.
2:10 a.m.	Stool. "Oh how my belly aches."
2:30	Refuses anything by mouth. Fixed another Opii injection, but can't get a chance to give it. Put fresh turpentine over abdomen. Abdomen is not swollen, but sunken. Face anxious, and appears to be in much pain often. Asked, "Is this our house?" Passed catheter in rectum while sleeping, but before could inject contents, she forced it out with stool.

---

[93] Opium.
[94] A baby talk for "food" in Korean.
[95] 2½ minims is about 2½ drops.

Journal of Edith Margaret Hall

3 a.m.	Was about to pass catheter again when she had another passage.
3:30 a.m.	Inserted catheter, but again it excited immediate bowel action. "Oh, how my stomach aches." Will not take anything. Feel she ought to have hypodermic to allay about her passages so much, but she has too much strength yet to allow one to do it properly alone without her consent. Just cries out with pain.
4 a.m.	Vomiting and retching. Bright bluish green vomit. More stools.
4:30 a.m.	Dr. Follwell injected Morphine gr 1/25
5 a.m.	Temperatures 99.4°.
5:15 a.m.	Valentine's Beef Juice ʒ ii Sol.
5:45 a.m.	Water.
6 a.m.	Water.
6:30 a.m.	Valentine's Sol ʒ ii.
7 a.m.	Valentine's Sol ʒ ii.
7:15 a.m.	First movement since morphine injection. Followed by 2 more before 7:30 a.m.
7:30 a.m.	Valentine's Beef juice ʒ ii Sol.
8:30 a.m.	Valentine's Beef juice ʒ ii Sol.
9:15 a.m.	Valentine's Beef juice ʒ ii Sol.
9:30 a.m.	Movement. Valentine's ʒ ii Sol.
10 a.m.	Opii gr 1/6 Salol gr ii, Ipecac gr ii.
10:15 a.m.	Vomited everything. Repeated it. Hypoderm gr 1/20.
10:30 a.m.	Salt water enema.
10:45 a.m.	Valentine's ʒ ii Sol. Movement. Slept most of the time till 12:45. Valentine's Sol.
1 p.m.	Movement.
2 p.m.	Valentine's ʒ i.
3:15 p.m.	Horlicks Food ℥ ii.
3:45 p.m.	Ipecac gr 1/5, Bismuth gr v.
4:15 p.m.	Vomited above without effort.
4:30 p.m.	Valentine's ʒ iv. Will give up ipecac.
5 p.m.	Bismuth and Salol.
5:15 p.m.	Morphine Hypoderm. Gr 1/20.
5:30 p.m.	Temperature 100.2°. Gave Valentine's ʒ ß[96].
6:45 p.m.	Tr. Opii ♏ iv in starch and Bismuth injection while sleeping.
7:30 p.m.	Stool, the first since 5 p.m. Couldn't see injection. The stools seem not so brightly bloody today. Darker and mixed with pus much as they did the 11th. Motions now followed up to 8:30 p.m. when she goes off of bedpan a short time. Then on it again till after Morphine Hypodermic.
7:30 p.m.	Beef juice ʒ ß with milk ʒ iii and water.
8:30 p.m.	Forced her to take a little more Valentine's solution and she vomited up over a cupful of brownish liquid.
9 p.m.	Vomited about one ounce the partly digested beef juice.

---

[96] Half dram.

Journal of Edith Margaret Hall

9:30 p.m.	Bismuch and Salol. Water.
10 p.m.	Temperature 102.4°. Sleeping on bedpan.
10:45 p.m.	Vomited again when taking beef solution.
11 p.m.	Hypoderm. of Morphine.
11:30 p.m.	Quiet. Gave Valentine's Solution ʒ ß.
11:40 p.m.	ʒ ß more.

Friday, May 13—

12:30 a.m.	Unusually restless, tossing and turning since 12 midnight. Rubbing herself here and there, must have a flea or a louse, or else it is an affect of the Morphine. Rubbed her abdomen with alcohol which she liked, but she kept on restlessly tossing afterward. Talked in her sleep—said, "Goodbye," and, "Sherwood, don't you want some of my medicine?" Asked for water—gave it. Said she wanted to "eugh and shee" but paid no attention to it. It is possible she should urinate and that is why she is so restless. Can't get a chance to give Opii and starch injection or take temperature.
1:30 a.m.	Gave Bismuth and Salol wet up in "meme." She spit it out. Gave it in powder and she swallowed it with water afterward. Still tossing—throwing herself first on her face then on her back—gets across the bed and every way. Said, "I am going to stay to prayers," "Did you set my house? I want to go to my house and play with Sherwood and Mary."
1:45 a.m.	"I want to eugh and shee." Couldn't put her off this time as I did an hour ago—the "eugh" came freely, but she can't urinate. Tried to pass my catheter but too large.
2 a.m.	Gave Valentine's Solution about ʒ ß. One more movement.
2:30 a.m.	Vomited freely again. Took 2 swallows of water after. Still restless. Called for "Dah"—repeated "Jesus loves me this I know." Asked for Dr. Harris. Feeling that urine must be gotten out—took a tiny baby catheter which as it was broken had thought I couldn't use, but in passing it, the urine flowed out freely of itself. About 3 ounces, acid.
3 a.m.	Gave Bismuth only—and water with 10 drops of Frumenti.
3:30 a.m.	Quieter, but now asks for bedpan, but couldn't take right away—movement quite large—mostly pus in globular masses. She seems quieter, but rolls about some and keeps arms up over her head. Wants to catch bees.
3:45 a.m.	Asked for cocoa—took one swallow of Horlicks Food. Probably noticed the difference though didn't say.
4:00 a.m.	Temperatures 101°, respiration 14. Not quite quiet yet and talks some in her sleep. Gave a little more water with Spts. of Frumenti ℞x.
4:30 a.m.	Involuntary stool, but asked for bedpan when she had finished, but didn't do more. Small stool mostly pus, some soft dark greenish masses. Water and Spts. Frumenti ℞x.

Journal of Edith Margaret Hall

4:40 a.m.	Another stool partly in napkin. Again complained of pain in abdomen—the first since 11 p.m.
4:45 a.m.	Bismuth, water and Spts. Frumenti ♏x. Has slept very lightly and very little since 11 p.m. Should have her other hypoderm now.
5:10 a.m.	Vomited the last given. Passed a little wind.
5:30 a.m.	Wants to vomit more. Pain. Movements continued. Said she'd let Mamma give the hypotherm. So Kumyongie[97] held arm. Sorry didn't give it an hour ago.
6 a.m.	Bismuth.
6:30 a.m.	Half cup cocoa. Still restless.
7:15 a.m.	Starch and Opii injection.
7:30 a.m.	Half cup cocoa and Horlicks Food.
8 a.m.	Half cup cocoa and Horlicks Food.
8:45 a.m.	Movement
9 a.m.	Temperature 101.2°, pulse 140.
9:10 a.m.	Cocoa and Horlicks Food ʒ ii.
10 a.m.	Bismuth. Movement.
10:30 a.m.	Morphine. Hypotherm.
10:30 a.m.	Movement. Cocoa and Horlicks ʒ i.
11:30 a.m.	Washed out bowels with Sodium Chloride.
12 noon	Temperature 100.3°.
12:25 p.m.	Stool.
1 p.m.	Cocoa and Horlicks.
1:15 p.m.	Bismuth gr v. Pulse 120, Respiration 14. Stool.
1:45 p.m.	A little Valentine's Solution. Stool.
2:15 p.m.	Bismuth and Salol. Passed urine (acid).
2:30 p.m.	Vomited. Movement.
2:45 p.m.	Water and Spts. of Frumenti.
3:10 p.m.	Stool, small.
3:40 p.m.	Vomited.
3:45 p.m.	Morphine gr 1/16, hypoderm.
4 p.m.	Temperature 100.3°. Stool.
4:30 p.m.	Bismuth gr v.
4:40 p.m.	Valentine's Solution.
5:40 p.m.	Valentine's Solution. Talks rather flighty but will answer sensibly when spoken to.
5:45 p.m.	Movement.
6:40 p.m.	Bovanine.
7:30 p.m.	Movement. A little water and Spts. Frumenti. Vomited. Talks a great deal.
8:30 p.m.	Washed out bowel with the Sodium Chloride and Ac. Carbol.[98]
8:45 p.m.	Morphine gr 1/16.

---

[97] Kumyong Yum (염금영) is house boy since Rosetta was in Seoul.
[98] **Ac'idum Carbol'icum.** — Carbolic Acid.

Journal of Edith Margaret Hall

9 p.m.	Temperature 102.4°.
9:45 p.m.	Cocoa.
10:15 p.m.	Movement. Could see quinine.
10:45 p.m.	Some Valentine's beef juice, a little cocoa.
11 p.m.	Sound of stool, but seemed nearer to be getting quiet than for a long time and let her be. She realizes something wrong though for she said, "I want to eugh, come quick, or I will eugh on my drawers."

May 13th continued—Has been restless all day, more or less, talks. Keeps eyes shut mostly. Seems still so strong. Keeps arms and hands moving. Often catches hold of those near her. Talked about "Nettie" twice. Said, "I don't want them children to come in here." Once wanted to get up and go and play with Ruth. When I left her this morning I said, "Kiss me"—at first she said "no." I told her I was going away now say good-bye. She said, "Goodbye." I said give me just one kiss; she said, "A dirty kiss or clean kiss?" I said a clean kiss of course, and she smacked her little lips, her eyes were shut and Mamma's face was not quite close enough to catch it, but that was Mamma's fault. Sometimes when she breathes through nose the nostrils move out and in. Her lips are drawn open, her teeth almost like a dead child's—eyes somewhat sunken, dark lids and about. Once she wanted Grandma to rub her back.

11:30 p.m. Quite quiet—the most like sleep I have seen for a day. Called out "Mama! Mama!" But when I went to her, pushed me away, saying her hands were dirty. Asked her if she would have some cocoa. Said no. Pulse 150, respiration 14.

12 midnight. Took a swallow of cocoa and Horlicks Food but nearly vomited. Fair looking stool. Inserted catheter and she urinated herself—acid—cloudy.

1 a.m. Vomited quite a quantity and seemed exhausted afterwards. Asked for water—gave it with Spts. Frumenti. She took it with relish and said, "That's good." Temperature 100.1°, pulse 180, respiration 12.

2 a.m. Vomited again—lies exhausted. Hardly know whether to give the morphine again or not—rather think she would have no more pain now, as she has not spoken of it even when coming out of the morphine now for some time. But as she would likely have to vomit a long time and perhaps have that dreadful skin irritation while coming out of it, perhaps it better be kept up a little longer till she keeps a bit more nourishment.

2:30 a.m. Gave the Hypoderm about 1/18 gr. Changed napkin—no blood, a fairly digested stool, little or no pus.

3 a.m. Edith is very quiet now, but will not take her cocoa that she wanted before the Hypoderm. But which I knew she'd vomit then. Fear heart is going but as it is still 180, has not slowed down from the morphine yet. It is fairly strong.

5:20 a.m. By this time got in Spts. in water 2 or 3 times and ½ cup cocoa and Horlicks Food and ½ ounce milk. She now wants to vomit for the first after the Hypoderm but didn't yet. Had foul stool.

5:30 a.m. Did vomit a little. Have decided to try stopping the morphine, as it keeps her such a short time without vomiting, and she needs such big doses.

Saturday, May 14, 1898

Up to noon of this day, vomited 4 times and had 4 stools. (No morphine). Had bowel washed out with salt water and gave enema of beef juice but did not retain it.

During afternoon, 3 stools and had bowels washed out again. Vomited 5 times. Began giving Carbolic Acid gr $1/6$ every 4 hours or so. Temperature 3 p.m. 99°, 7 p.m. 100.3°, pulse 144.

Had bed changed and clean shirt and gown today. Took little lemonade. Vomited 14 times during this 24 hours. Pain before and during stools much increased and had 21 movements. Pulse grew very weak and compressible during night. Gave stimulants. Could take very little food as she was so nauseated.

Sunday, May 15, 1898

As the vomiting and pain continued during the morning, decided to try giving her an opiate again for it and to allay inflammation of bowels. At 3:30 gave Opii gr ¼ and Ipecac gr $1/60$ which was repeated every 3 hours. Only vomited once after for about 12 hours. But stools not yet controlled. They contain more bright blood and tissue again, instead of pus, and it would seem as if a new portion of bowel was becoming involved. She rests more quietly under the opium than the morphine, and would likely be much improved, if more bowel had not broken down. Had 30 stools during the 24 hours and vomited 7 times. Temperature ran up to 101° again. Pulse 140.

Journal of Edith Margaret Hall

Monday, May 16, 1898

Has less pain today and rests more quietly. Stools contain a little food and spinach-looking material sometimes, but still bloody serum and a blood clot or two. Takes nourishment better. Milk with barley gruel and lime water, and sometimes Bovanine. Valentine beef juice all gone and can get no mutton to make broth of here, and it is not safe to use the beef. She sometimes asks for cocoa and takes quite a little made with Horlicks milk. Opium and Ac. Carbol. treatment continued. Bowels washed out once daily with salt and a little Ac. Carbol. Temperature kept 101° all day running up to 103° at 1 p.m. It would seem there has been a complication of malaria. Probably continued malarial fever. Didn't begin to note temperature until the 12th, so it is not clear. During this 24 hours had only 10 stools and didn't vomit at all which seems a decided improvement in all except the temperature. Respiration has increased from 14 under the morphine and opium at first to 24 and 26 which indicate some catarrhal involvement of lungs also, which might occur in connection with the continued malarial fever. Pulse 153 to 190 (though Dr. Follwell count it lower) generally. Began inunctioning[99] of quinine in cream, rubbing over sides, stomach and thigh particularly, and later rubbing off with alcohol. She seems to absorb quite a little of it.

Tuesday, May 17, 1898

Less tenesmus. Knows when she is done with movement and will let bedpan be removed more readily. Some stools contain quite a little food partly formed. Took ʒ iv–vi of food every 2 hours. Other treatment continued. Had 15 stools and did not vomit. Temperature went up to 102° though.

Wednesday, May 18, 1898

Lessened the Opii to gr 1/5 every 3 hours. Coat beginning to peel off tongue—it was heavy brown black in middle. She picks it off some herself and like her mouth washed out now and then. She urinates 2 to 3 times in 24 hours but have to pass or partly pass catheter first, then she urinates freely herself about 3 ounces. Had 19 stools. Sometimes bloody mucus, sometimes a little digested food or spinach green. Vomited only once. Lies on her back altogether now except when turned, and then at first has to cough and have some difficulty breathing before she can

---

[99] the rubbing of ointments into the pores of the skin, by which medicinal agents contained in them, such as mercury, iodide of potash, etc., are absorbed.

get adjusted to the change. Is getting pretty thin, but no bed sore. Had 1 gr quinine sulphate by mouth.

Thursday, May 19, 1898

Had 5 gr quinine sulphate in Syrup of Glycerine—took it well, gr I or gr ii at a time. Complained of stomach ache again. Stools more foul again, charred looking with pus—or spinach with pus. Temperature went up to 103.6°. Had 18 stools and didn't vomit. Seemed decidedly weaker tonight.

Friday, May 20, 1898

Coat about all off of tongue, but it is hard, raw and sore—a weak listerine wash bites it. Had 7 gr quinine sulphate today and began giving Tr. Ferri Chlor. ♏ii. Her temperature kept down, but stomach began to give out again—vomited 3 times. Stools 15. Begin giving Opii gr 1/8, Ipecac gr 1/16 and Lead acetate gr 1/12, Camphor gr 1/8 at noon in place of the other Opii powder but is more nauseated again and will not eat well. Stools vary, but yet blood clots now and then with pus and nearly always the bloody serum and spinach green.

Saturday, May 21, 1898

Had 5 gr quinine sulphate and temperature kept down to 100° nearly all day, but rose toward morning with symptoms of local peritonitis. 13 stools. Vomited 3 times. Breathing much more oppressed. She feels badly. Has done involuntary stool sometimes, brownish-black, foul. Don't talk but frets and grunts out expirations[100]. Complaining of pain in abdomen again. Axilla getting so thin, can hardly hold thermometer. Keeps both knees up, now most of the time—likes her belly gently rubbed—it is fuller now, but not much swollen. She seems so weak, difficult to understand her. Asked twice for lemonade. Modified Opii and lead mixture, less Ipecac and more Opii.

---

[100] Exhalation of breath.

Journal of Edith Margaret Hall

Sunday, May 22, 1898

When given food, would insist that they should "keep it for tomorrow days." At noon moved her to Mrs. Lee's guesthouse and she liked the change, and seemed rather better for a time. More restful.

Continued to apply Turpentine on flannel to abdomen. She sometimes rests with knees down, but still likes them up. Gave iron but she generally vomited it. Didn't dare try the quinine yet again. Gave nourishment ʒ ii to iv every half hour. Milk, barley and Bovanine, alternating with chicken broth—continued it through night. Had 14 stools and vomited 4 times. At 3:30 in the morning seemed to be suffering much again—rolling head uneasily from side to side. Anxious look upon brow, lips white. Picks at her lips and teeth where for the last 24 hours sordes will collect upon her teeth. For nearly 2 hours continued uneasy, and moaning out now and then, "That's enough." Took ʒ iii of nourishment every half hour with her brother's tiny spoon.

Slept quite quietly from 5:20 a.m. to 6:30 a.m. Gave some chicken broth. Rubbed with alcohol and changed clothes by degrees. She laid about half hour upon right side and seemed quite comfortable. Her temperature ran up to 102.4° but came down 0.6° after her alcohol bath.

Monday, May 23, 1898

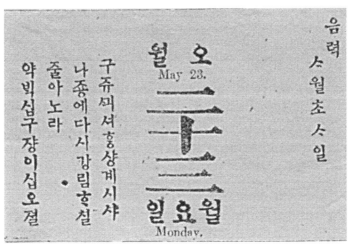

"음력 ᄉ월초ᄉ일, 오월 二十三 일요일, Monday, May 23, 1898, 구쥬씌셔호샹계시샤나죵에다시강림ᄒ실줄아노라 야빅십구쟝이십오절"[101]

Asked to be rocked almost for the first since she was sick. Urinated herself twice before noon without help. Had 7 stools and vomited 7 times from 8 a.m. to 8 p.m. She asked for cocoa frequently and sometimes for water—would take ʒ ii or iii at a time. Her stools from early

---

[101] "Lunar calendar April 4, Monday, May 23, 1898. For I know that my redeemer liveth, and that he shall stand at the latter day upon the earth. Job 19:25 (KJV)"

morning changed in character—containing little and sometimes no blood—seemed diarrhea—brown liquids. At 3 p.m., her hands and feet were cold—face and body hot. Temperature 103.2°. Had another alcohol bath and hot water balls at feet.

5:05 p.m.	Temperature was 104. Had a dose of antifebrin and it went down to 103.1° (?).
6:45 p.m.	Restless and sighing. Nauseated.
7:15 p.m.	Temperature 100.5°.
7:30 p.m.	Hypodermic Spts. Frumenti ℳx.
7:50 p.m.	Vomited for the last time what appears to be Bovanine.
8 p.m.	Sucked with relish a little ice cream from brother's little spoon. (Her brin was left at Mrs. Nobles) She took several tiny spoon's full this way and was not nauseated anymore.
8:25 p.m.	Temperature 106°, respiration 52, difficult. Mamma took her in her arms and rocked her like she used to when going to take her afternoon nap. She breathed much more quietly, seemed content. Her face became peaceful, her breaths farther and farther apart, and with wide-open eyes looking into Mamma's her little spirit wended its way back to the God who gave it at 8:40 p.m., Monday, May 23, 1898.

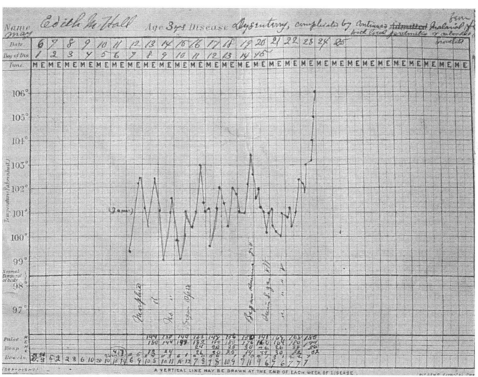

Medical record of Edith's vital signs during her illness.
"Edith M. Hall, age 3 years, disease:
Dysentery, complicated by continued malarial fever with local peritonitis and catarrhal bronchitis.
May 6 – 23, 1898."

Notes

Often when she has to "eugh" as she calls it so often, Edith will say, "Oh, I am so soddy—so soddy." Once she said, "Sherwood is soddy too." Sometimes she says, "I am awful soddy," when she vomits her nice food. When she doesn't care to take all of what is offered her, she says, "Save it for tomorrow days," or, "Don't throw it away." She asks sometimes if her face is clean. One time when under the morphia, which seemed to make her a little contrary by the way, Mamma said, "Edith, do you love Mama?" "Yes." "Do you love Jesus?" "No." "Oh, yes you do." "No I don't. I love you, I like you, but I don't like Jesus." Another time when out of the morphia Mamma said, "Does Jesus love little Edith?" "Yes," she said without hesitation. "Does Edith love Jesus?" "Yes," plain and clear. One time when asked if she thought she was going to get well, she said, "Yes, God is making me better." Night of the 16th the best she has had, Edith said when rubbing her with alcohol, "You are a good Mamma," just as she so often used to state when well. When asked who else she loved beside Mamma, she said, "I love Gamma, and I love Dah, and I love black Joe." "Do you love Sherwood?" "Yes." "Papa?" "Yes." "Jesus?" "Yes." "God?" "Yes." Toward morning when awakened to take her medicine, she said, "I saw Mary play ring-a-round-rosy down at the hospital." She once asked for toast, and once for chicken in the night. It has been her best night, and Mamma feels encouraged again, and so thankful if God's will be to spare the comforter. He so kindly sent her, when He took Papa away.

Morning of May 17th enjoyed her morning wash.

Morning of May 18th, pointed to "Bible Society Gleanings" that lay on bed and said, "I want that." She took it and looked at pictures, also fanned herself, and seemed more natural. May 18th, just 3 years 4 months today. When she vomited early this morning, the first for some time she said it was "because she ate that Korean food."

May 21, nausea and retching worse. Wants to "keep" all her food "for tomorrow days."

May 22, after taking a little taste of gelatin said, "That jelly hurts me." May 22, Sunday noon moved her upon Mr. Noble's cottage to Mrs. Lee's guest house by invitation. Thinking it would be beneficial to the malaria especially. She stood the change well and appreciated it. Looked about her and noticed everything so fresh and clean and sweet. She seemed more restful 5:30 p.m. Wanted Mamma to lay her head down on her pillow and go to sleep with her.

May 23rd early morning, from 3:30 to 5:20, was so uneasy, rolling head from side-to-side, picking at teeth and lips. Seemed to be suffering with such an anxious look upon her. Dear little face, her brow so troubled and perplexed. She begged Mamma to hold her, but as long as there was any hope, at all, Mamma feared to do it, for her heart was so very weak, and any change of position was likely to make her vomit, or have difficult restoration. She grunts out her expirations—and moans a little, saying now and then, "That's enough."

About 10 a.m., Mamma placed some white dandelions in her hand which she enjoyed and held for a long time. Mamma then went to lie down and Grandma Webb raised Edith, Drs. Wells and Follwell, one or the other being present most of the time. Sometimes when she didn't want to take her food or medicine if Mrs. Webb would say take it for "Grandma," she would take it; that word appealed to her, and the last conscious reply she made was to the question, "Do you love Grandma?" about 3 hours before she passed away. The last thing she asked for was for cocoa at 2:45 p.m.—it was ever her standby as food. Soon after 8 p.m. Mamma "byed" her darling in her arms to her last long sleep.

> "We shall sleep but not forever, in the lone and silent grave
> Blessed be the Lord that taketh, blessed be the Lord that gave."[102]

---

[102] Mary Ann Pepper Kidder (1820-1905).

The Last Journey

By Francis Barine

The little traveler set forth
   With one last smile of sweet content.
There are no footprints, south or north,
   To show to us the way she went;
No tiny footprints in the snow,
   No flower for token backward thrown.
"Sweetheart," we wept, "why must you go?"
   Smiling, she went her way, alone.

The little traveler went her way
   And left us all who loved her so.
She journeyed forth at break of day—
   A long, long way she had to go.
The stars were paling in the sky—
   Their kind eyes must have seen her start.
We could not see; we could but cry,
   "Come back to us, dear heart, dear heart!"

The little traveler's tiny feet
   Have found a path that we must find.
She was so little and so sweet!
   We cannot linger, left behind.
We stumble, seeking, day by day.
   O little traveler, who will send
A guide to point us out the way
   To find you at the journey's end?

Journal of Edith Margaret Hall

Grandma's last letter to Edith, received after her "Little Tot" had gone.

Grandma's letter received after Edith's death

My Little Tot,

I was so glad to get your letter. Did you know you have a little Cousin at your Aunt Annie's? Her name is Nelly, and they have two little baby kittens. If you were there, you could have a nice time playing with them and you have a Cousin here, a little boy isn't named, talk of calling him Ralph. How I would like to see you all, to make you a visit. You mustn't forget me. Joe often talks of you; he will send you a card before long. Goodbye. God bless us. Grandma

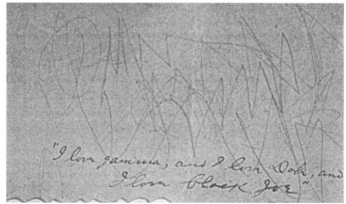

A piece of the last letter Edith wrote to Grandma, written May 9, 1898:
"I love gamma, and I love Dah, and I love black Joe."

Telegram to Dr. Hall in "Pingyang" from W. F. M. S.: "Isaiah forty-three two."
"Fear not for I redeem you, I claim you, you are mine.
I will be with you when you through waters, no rivers shall overflow you;
when you pass through fire you shall not be scorched, no flames shall burn you."

Rev. and Mrs. Graham Lee's guest house, Pyong Yang, where Edith passed away, May 23, 1898.

Journal of Edith Margaret Hall

Wednesday, May 25, 1898

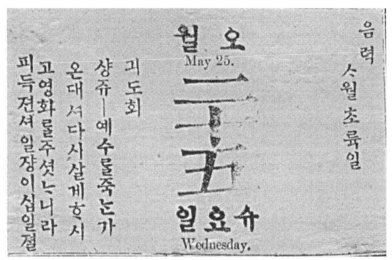

"음력 ᄉᆞ월초륙일, 오월 二十五 슈요일, Wednesday, May 25, 1898, 긔도회 샹쥬— 예수를죽는가온대셔다시살게ᄒᆞ시고영화를주섯ᄂᆞ니라 피득젼셔 일쟝이십일졀"[103]

**The funeral service at the home of a Rev. Graham Lee,
Wednesday afternoon, May 25, 1898**

Hymn, [blank]

Scripture, Ezek. 24:16-17, 25-27. (Selected by Mamma)

Behold, I take away from thee the desire of thine eyes with a stroke: yet neither shalt thou mourn nor weep, neither shall thy tears run down. Forbear to cry, make no mourning for the dead, bind the tire of thine head upon thee, and put on thy shoes upon thy feet, and cover not thy lips, and eat not the bread of men. Also, shall it not be in the day when I take from them their strength, the joy of their glory, the desire of their eyes, and that whereupon they set their minds, their sons and their daughters, ++ In that day shall thy mouth be opened, ++ and thou shalt speak, and be no more dumb: and thou shalt be a sign unto them; and they shall know that I *am* the LORD.

Heb. 4: 15-16 (Selected by Mr. Noble)

---

[103] Lunar calendar April 6, Wednesday, May 25, 1898. Who by him do believe in God, that raised him up from the dead, and gave him glory; that your faith and hope might be in God. I Peter 1:21."

For we have not a high priest which cannot be touched with the feeling of our infirmities; ++ Let us therefore come boldly unto the throne of grace, that we may obtain mercy, and find grace to help in time of need.

Also Matt. 19:13-15.

Hymn, "Jesus Loves Me"— Edith's favorite

Ballad of Baby Bell (Aldrich)[104], Read by Mrs. Noble

Have you not heard the poets tell
How came the dainty Baby Bell
Into this world of ours?
The gates of heaven were left ajar;
With folded hands and dreamy eyes,
Wandering out of Paradise,
She saw this planet, like a star,
Hung in the glistening depths of even, —
Its bridges, running to and fro,
O'er which the white-winged angels go,
Bearing the holy dead to heaven.
She touched a bridge of flowers, — those feet,
So light they did not bend the bells
Of the celestial asphodels!
They fell like dew upon the flowers,
Then all the air grew strangely sweet!
And thus came dainty Baby Bell
Into this world of ours.

O Baby, dainty Baby Bell,
How far she grew from day to day!
What woman-nature filled her eyes,
What poetry within them lay!
Those deep and tender twilight eyes,
So full of meaning, pure and bright,
As if she yet stood in the light
Of those opened gates of Paradise.
And so we loved her more and more;
Ah, never in our hearts before
Was love so lovely born:
We felt we had a link between

---

[104] Thomas Bailey Aldrich (1836–1907).

This real world and that unseen —
The land beyond the morn.

God's hand had taken away the seal
That held the portals of her speech;
And oft she said a few strange words
Whose meaning lay beyond our reach.
She never was a child to us,
We never held her being's key,
We could not teach her holy things;
She was Christ's self in purity.

It came upon us by degrees,
We saw its shadow ere it fell:
The knowledge that our God had sent
His messenger for Baby Bell.
We shuddered with unlanguaged pain,
And all our hopes were changed to fears,
And all our thoughts ran into tears
Like sunshine into rain.
We cried aloud in our belief,
"Oh, smite us gently, gently, God!
Teach us to bend and kiss the rod,
And perfect grow through grief."
Ah, how we loved her, God can tell;
Her heart was folded deep in ours.
Our hearts are broken, Baby Bell!

At last he came, the messenger,
The messenger from unseen lands:
And what did dainty Baby Bell?
She only crossed her little hands;
She only looked more meek and fair!
We parted back her silken hair,
We wove the roses round her brow, —
White buds, the summer's drifted snow, —
Wrap her from head to foot in flowers!
And then went dainty Baby Bell
Out of this world of ours!

Address to the Koreans, by Rev. William B. Baird

Solo, "Some Sweet Day"—Rev. Graham Lee

Address, by Rev. W. A. Noble (who had the service in charge)

Burial Service

Hymn, "We Shall Sleep But Not Forever"

Benediction, Mr. Lee

Thursday, May 26, 1898

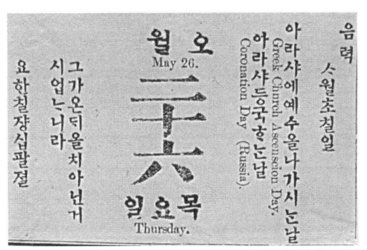

"음력 ᄉ월초칠일, 오월 二十六 목요일, Thursday, May 26, 1898, 아라샤에예수올나가시ᄂ날 Greek Church Ascenscion Day. 아라샤등국ᄒ눈날 Coronation Day (Russia). 그가온듸올치아닌거시업ᄂ니라 요한칠쟝십팔졀"[105]

    It was Mamma's wish that the precious body of her baby daughter might be laid at rest by Papa's. Mr. Lee kindly soldered of tin an air tight box, and accompanied by faithful Kim Chang Sikey the little body of the dear child her Papa never saw in this life made the long overland journey to Söul that he had so often made, leaving Pyong Yang May 26th and reaching there June 1st. The following extract from Rev. H. G. Appenzeller's letter tells the rest.

    "At noon yesterday, as I came down from School, I found Brother Kim at my door. I was prepared to see him as I had learned that you proposed as was quite natural and evidently proper to have little Edith buried by her Papa in our Cemetery here. ++ Miss Pierce brought a bunch of white peonies, my wife sent a wreath of white roses, and Alice

---

[105] Lunar calendar April 7, Thursday, May 26, 1898, Greek Church Ascenscion Day, Coronation Day (Russia). And no unrighteousness is in him. John 7:18."

made a Cross of white roses. These we laid upon the coffin as it rested over the open grave. I read the words "I am the resurrection and the life," and we sang in Korean "Asleep in Jesus, Blessed Sleep." The flowers were then removed, and Brother Bunker, Swearer, Kim and myself lowered the coffin, after which I read our beautiful burial service, and called on Rev. Kim to lead in prayer followed by the Lord's Prayer in concert. The whole was a beautiful, simple impressive service, such as I know you would have liked. The mound was heaped up, and the flowers placed on top. Your dear little girl sleeps now by her father's bosom, and the two will rise again at the call of the last trumpet. Half of your Family is in Heaven."

Mama has received many precious letters of tender sympathy from which she would like to make extracts here, and perhaps can sometime, but other duties have so far forbidden. Even these words have had to be written long after.

"And this is the end of it all!
Of my waiting and my pain—
Only a little funeral pall
And empty arms again."

My heart is near to break
For the voice I shall not hear,
For the clinging arms about my neck,
And the footsteps drawing near.

For the precious Mother-name,
And the touch of the little hand,
O! am I so very much to blame
If I shrink from the sore demand?

And this is the end of it all!
Of my waiting and my pain—
Only a little funeral pall,
And empty arms again.[106]

Like a cradle, rocking, rocking
    Silent, peaceful, to and fro,
Like a mother's sweet looks dropping
    On the little face below—
Hangs the green earth, swinging, turning,
    Jarless, noiseless, safe and slow;
Falls the light of God's face bending
    Down and watching us below.

And as feeble babes that suffer,
    Toss and cry, and will not rest,
Are the ones the tender mother
    Holds the closest, loves the best;
So when we are weak and wretched,
    By our tears[107] weighed down, distressed,
Then it is that God's great patience
    Holds us closest, loves us best.

O great heart of God! whose loving
    Cannot hindered be nor crossed;
Will not weary, will not even
    In our death itself be lost;
Love divine! of such great loving
    Only mothers know the cost—
Cost of love, which all love passing,
    Gave a Son to save the lost.   —Saxe Holm

---

[106] From "My Baby," anonymous.
[107] Rosetta changed "sins" to "tears."

Wednesday, January 18, 1899

Eye hath not seen, not ear heard, neither have entered into the heart of man, the things which God hath prepared for them that love him. I Cor. 2:9

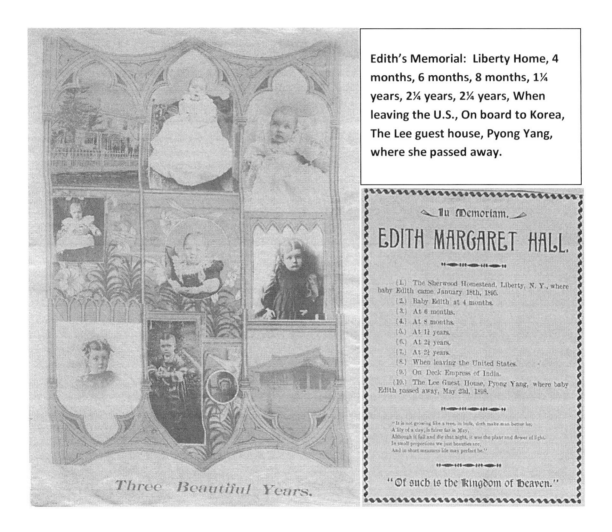

"Short was her earthly course, and soon
    Loosed was the silver cord,
Loosed but on earth, for a golden tie
    United it to God."   —Henrietta Hook, 1850

Journal of Edith Margaret Hall

A year ago when Mamma wrote of the first birthday her darling spent in Korea, she had no thought the next one would be spent in heaven. When she was a wee baby she was not very well, and others sometimes thought she could not live; but Mamma always felt God would not take away her "little comforter" so graciously sent in her time of need. And later, by the time she had grown a year old she was so sturdy and vigorous that no one apprehended any danger for her. Sherwood had his spells of poor appetite, but Edith was always ready for her meals, and was never sick to speak of until she had the catarrhal pneumonia at Chemulpo; but she made a normal recovery from it and was very well until she has the measles. After that, she was not quite so well—had quite a severe ear-ache with fever once and another time a phlyctenular conjunctivitis which let Mamma know she was a little run down; but Mamma thought when she got her in a home of her own where she could sit at the table with Mamma, and Mamma could control her diet better, she would soon be well and strong again, but alas! that time never came. Mamma cannot help regretting a number of things, but it is of no avail.

It seems as if Mamma needs her little comforter, more and more each day, and brother needs her more. We <u>do need</u> her, there is no question about that, but for some wise reason we cannot now understand, God thought best to deprive us of her.

I think Mamma did not record last winter about how much interest Edith took in the sick folks, especially the children. After her afternoon nap she often came into the dispensary before Mamma got quite through with the patients. At night to her "Now I lay me" was often added such a petition as this, "God bless the little babies at the hospital what's got the little bite of head and one has sore eyes." If a tooth had to be drawn or an abscess lanced Sherwood was always quick enough to run away, but she stood her ground unless sent away. One afternoon she came in when Mamma was so busy with an operation she did not notice her. Some blood had spattered on Mamma's face, Edith saw Mary Hoang, sponging blood with some cotton, so procuring some, she placed a stool in position, and climbing up began to wipe the blood from Mammas face! She was ever so helpful, so brave and prompt in action that Mamma felt sure she would make a physician herself someday.

Edith had a little pocket-book that Joe gave her, and she was trying to save her money; she never had nearly so much given her as Sherwood, but when she died she had altogether $2.12 ½ (gold); to this Mamma added nearly $25 more the proceeds from stock of new goods for Edith. (All her best clothes that she had worn were sent to "baby Julia,"[108] and all the rest were given to children in Pyong Yang.) Mama thought it would be good to devote this money toward building some wards for little Korean children, as a memorial for her little daughter. She spoke of it in some of her home letters, and hoped to have a little added to it by some of the

---

[108] See the diary of October 23, 1897.

home friends, but was surprised when last night mail brought a check for no less than $150 gold for this purpose. It seemed like a birthday present for Edith, and that is what suggested the Bible verse for today. If she receives such a present on earth, what may she not receive in Heaven? This check was from Cousin Polly Crary, her daughter Emma Young, and granddaughters Louise and Polly Young. They have decided instead of giving each other their customary Christmas gifts to send the money for this memorial.

"SOME TIME."

MRS. MAY RILEY SMITH.

Some time, when all life's lessons have been learned,
   And sun and stars forevermore have set,
The things which our weak judgment here has spurned—
   The things o'er which we grieved with lashes wet—
Will flash before us out of life's dark night,
   As stars shine most in deeper tints of blue;
And we shall see how all God's plans were right,
   And how what seemed reproof was love most true.

And we shall see, that, while we frown and sigh,
   God's plans go on as best for you and me;
How, when we called He heeded not our cry,
   Because His wisdom to the end could see:
And e'en as prudent parents disallow
   Too much of sweet to craving babyhood,
So God, perhaps, is keeping from us now
   Life's sweetest things, because it seemeth good.

And if, some time, commingled with life's wine,
   We find the wormwood, and rebel and shrink,
Be sure a wiser hand than yours or mine
   Pours out this potion for our lips to drink;
And if some friend we love is lying low,
   Where human kisses cannot reach his face,
Oh! do not blame the loving Father so,
   But bear your sorrow with obedient grace.

And you shall shortly know that lengthened breath
   Is not the sweetest gift God sends His friend,
And that sometimes the sable pall of death
   Conceals the fairest boon His love can send.
If we could push ajar the gates of life,
   And stand within, and all God's working's see,
We could interpret all this doubt and strife,
   And for each mystery could find a key.

But not to-day. Then be content, poor heart!
   God's plans, like lilies pure and white, unfold;
We must not tear the close-shut leaves apart;
   Time will reveal the calyxes of gold.
And if, through patient toil we reach the land
   Where tired feet, with sandals loosed, may rest,
When we shall clearly know and understand,
   I think that we shall say that "God knew best."

"Some Time" by Mrs. May Riley Smith

Some Time
Mrs. May Riley Smith

Some time, when all life's lessons have been learned,
And sun and stars forevermore have set,
The things which our weak judgment here has spurned—
The things o'er which we grieved with lashes wet—
Will flash before us out of life's dark night,
As stars shine most in deeper tints of blue;
And we shall see how all God's plans were right,
And how what seemed reproof was love most true.

And we shall see, that, while we frown and sigh,
God's plans go on as best for you and me;
How, when we called He heeded not our cry,
Because His wisdom to the end could see:
And e'en as prudent parents disallow
Too much of sweet to craving babyhood,
So God, perhaps, is keeping from us now
Life's sweetest things, because it seemeth good.

And if, some time, commingled with life's wine,
We find the wormwood, and rebel and shrink,
Be sure a wiser hand than yours or mine
Pours out this potion for our lips to drink;
And if some friend we love is lying low,
Where human kisses cannot reach his face,
Oh! Do not blame the loving Father so,
But bear your sorrow with obedient grace.

And you shall shortly know that lengthened breath
Is not the sweetest gift God sends His friend,
And that sometimes the sable pall of death
Conceals the fairest boon His love can send.
If we could push ajar the gates of life,
And stand within, and all God's working's see,
We could interpret all this doubt and strife,
And for each mystery could find a key.

But not today. Then be content, poor heart!
God's plans, like lilies pure and white, unfold;
We must not tear the close-shut leaves apart;
Time will reveal the calyxes of gold.
And if, through patient toll we reach the land
Where tired feet, with sandals loosed, may rest,
When we shall clearly know and understand,
I think that we shall say that "God knew best."

When we left America dear Grandma gave Mamma $5 for each child with a direction to use a dollar each year for Christmas or birthday presents. As a gold dollar makes two silver yen, one could be used for Christmas and one for birthday. After Edith's death Mamma put the Christmas money in with that set apart for the Children's wards, and she decided to use the birthday money each year to make a little party for Korean girls of Edith's age. She had already bought the candy and cake, and a little toy for each to take one, and had sufficient left to buy for vermicelli soup and add a poached egg to each bowl in the morning; and she was thinking about what she would say to the children, wondering if among other things she my speak of this plan for a Children's wards and ask them to pray for it, but it seemed as if it would take so long to get sufficient money, that she just decided to wait till next year before she spoke to them about it when this letter with the $150 came, and she felt so rebuked for lack of faith she fell upon her knees at once in a prayer of confession and thanksgiving, and of course, the little Korean girls and their mothers heard about the Children's wards today.

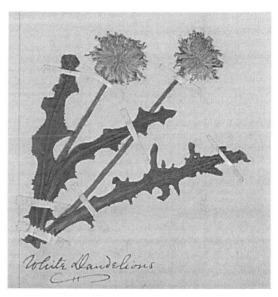

White Dandelions

Ruth Noble and her mamma were also here. Beside the things already mentioned which were all bought with the silver yen, we had popcorn and Japanese oranges. The children all had a happy time, and it gave Mamma and Sherwood pleasure to see them enjoy themselves, though our pleasure was mixed with sadness. Grandma too will be pleased the money was used this way, and will be glad to hear it so used each year. Dear Grandma, she misses her baby surely. She wrote "to tell you the truth I never saw a child (outside of my own) that I loved as I did Edith." She always calls her "my little Tot." She says, "I feel so lonesome without her, and I think of her often in the night as well as in the day." She sometimes speaks of seeing other "little Tots" that reminds her of "ours."

Tuesday, May 23, 1899

For He knoweth ++; He remembereth. Psa. 103:14

Once more the little white clovers have come
    Dotting the meadows green;
I wish I could tell you out of my heart
    What the little white clovers mean.

I had a sweet babe one year ago
    A 'dark-haired'[109] darling grace;
I see this moment those azure eyes
    And the little dimpled face;

The tiny feet that wandered about
    I have the shoes that covered them yet
And I hear her laugh, as in and out
    Through the grass her footsteps met.

The meadow and lane and garden were full
    Of blossoms sweet and gay
She always gathered white clover-heads
    And threw the rest away.

And when her little breathless form
    Was 'robed for her long last sleep,'[110]
There were clover-heads in her dainty hands—
    'Hands that could no more clovers reap.'[111]

How long it seems since I saw her last
    'My darling, Edith Margaret'[112];
And I wonder oft 'if as of yore
    My baby thinks of her mother yet?'[113]

If when I come to the pearly gate
    My darling will meet me there;
And if she will know me, grown so old
    With the silver in my hair!

The little white clover-heads bear me a song.
    Floating down from the chairs above,
Of the 'picture of hope'[114], the triumph of faith
    And the comfort of heavenly love;

Of the tender touch of grace divine
    That healeth my stricken heart,
Of the joy of the glad resurrection morn

---

[109] Rosetta changed "golden-haired" to "dark-haired" to match Edith's hair color.
[110] Original: "laid away under the hill."
[111] Original: "her hands so cold and still."
[112] Original: "But my darling I never forget."
[113] In a separate clip, Rosetta wrote: "if my baby Edith remembers her mother yet."
[114] Original: "patience of hope."

And the never-more-to-part.

The homely field-flowers I love full well
    Though naught to many who see
But the little white clovers, as long as I live,
    Will be dearest of all to me.

—Adapted from Mrs. Helen E. Brown, "White-Clovers and White-Dandelions"

Mamma and Sherwood being in Söul, were privileged to visit Papa's and Edith's graves today. How much those two green mounds take out of our lives here below; but He knoweth, He remembereth, like as a father pitieth his children, the Lord pities us—and we may be sure that he chastens us in love. "O Thou that hearest prayer,"[115] grant that we may be so exercised by this grievous chastening, that it may yield the "peaceable fruit of righteousness"[116] that thou doest design.

Tuesday, January 18, 1900

Let us not love in word, neither in tongue; but in deed and in truth. I John 3:18

"Every life is meant to help all lives; each man should live for all men's betterment." — Alice Cary

"I cannot do much" said a little star,
    "To make this dark world bright;
My silvery beams cannot pierce far
    Into the gloom of night;
Yet I am a part of God's great plan,
    And so I will do the best that I can."   —Margaret E. Sangster

This is the fifth anniversary of Edith's birth, and we celebrated it as last year by inviting little Korean girls of her age to a little treat with Grandma's birthday dollar. Seven were invited, and six came; as the mother or grandmother accompanied each, with Susan and Sherwood it made quite a party.

---

[115] Psalm 65:2.
[116] Hebrews 12:11.

Although the Edith Margaret Children's Wards are not finished yet, two rooms and the kitchen have been completed enough for use this winter, and it seemed so nice to be able to have our little party here this year. It seems wonderful that what we scarcely dared to hope for one year ago is so nearly accomplished already. Susan occupies one of the pleasant rooms and here they all met. When all had gathered we passed into the other room, Children's Ward No. 1, which has a large crayon of Edith in a handsome gilt frame hung upon the wall, and some of her toys upon the shelf. A low table with a white table-cloth was set with pretty tea-plates for each Child, and there were small colored glass dishes filled with bright Japanese candy for each child to carry away as a souvenir. This year all were served with bread, crackers, Japanese cakes, and catnip tea with sugar. Then there was plenty of Korean candy, popcorn and peanuts. Each child was given a paper bag in which to carry some home, and all had a good time. One little blind girl especially enjoyed herself, and the little glass dish proved a pleasure that lasted for days after—in fact in a number of the homes where I called later I found the little glass dish the treasure that each child hugged up to her when she went to sleep at night after playing with it all day.

With Edith's picture looking down at us, the children and their mothers listened to the story of why we celebrated this day, and of the birthday dollar, and of how wonderfully God has answered our prayers of a year ago, and gave us this pleasant building to meet in. We sang Edith's favorite song "Jesus Loves Me" and "There is a Happy Land," and I feel all were uplifted by our afternoon together.

The picture of the building on the other page was taken by one of our native Christians; it gives a fair idea of the building in its present unfinished state. Before another year we hope to have a better picture showing it all completed. Cold weather came on last fall before we could do more, also the funds were all exhausted; but there is promise of some more already, Sherwood gave his Christmas dollar, and one that was given him at the mines[117], also 500 cash part of which he had earned carrying brick on his *jiggy*[118] and the rest had been given by patients to him, and we will probably have more to give later between us. In a recent letter from Rev. D. M. Powell he spoke of Edith and Sherwood when they were there burying a little dead bird behind their barn; and then he added

> "Poor little Edith we often think of her and talk of her brave prompt ways. She seemed so different from little Sherwood, he seemed more frail; she was so well and evinced by her speech and act such a rugged constitution, that it seemed strange that she should be taken from earth to the home above, when this world needs so much just such a brave rugged natures as she gave promise of furnishing."

---

[117] Unsan Gold Mines.
[118] *Jigae* – an A-frame carrier.

So Mamma is not the only one who saw promise of great usefulness in her little daughter.

It seems as if Mamma misses Edith more than ever this winter.

"Fer at night time a feller feels lonesome,
Jest a-longin', you understand,
Fer the kiss of a prattlin' baby, the tetch of
A little hand."

Sherwood, too, talks more of her, and seems to miss her more than before. Life seems so hard without her.

"'Only a baby!' Ah! Do you not know
That little feet walk where no others can go
    That soft little fingers
        Lard on the chords
    Make music that lingers
        Sweeter than words?
That the touch of a baby has magic that brings
Harmonies rich from discordant heartstrings?"

The Edith Margaret Children's Wards

Journal of Edith Margaret Hall

Wednesday, May 23, 1900

A voice was heard in Ramah, lamentation and bitter weeping; Rahel weeping for her children refused to be comforted for her children, because they were not. Jer. 31:15

The's a good many different sorts an' kinds o' sorro' that in some ways kind o' kin to each other, but I guess losin' a child's a specia by itself. +++ The's some sorr' that the hapenin' o' things helps ye to fergit, I guess the's some that the happenin' o' things keeps ye rememberin; an lisin' or child's one on 'em. —From *David Harum*[119]

This day finds Mamma and Sherwood at Shanghai, China. Our darling Edith has been gone two long years, and as we see Ruth and Gretchen, and Mary, we can't help but to wonder what she would have been like now. She would no doubt have been taller than Sherwood for she was nearly 2 inches taller than he was at three years of age. Her dark hair would have been long again by this time, and her dear baby face would be that of a beautiful little girl, for Edith was ever changing for the better in looks, and even when we went to Pyong Yang Mrs. Noble pronounced to her beautiful. Mamma is sure also that Edith would have been a very helpful child by this time—no doubt dressing and undressing herself, and even helping brother. She would read and write Korean like he does, and recite Bible verses, and no doubt sing little songs like Gretchen, for dear Grandma said she thought Edith would sing easier than Sherwood. What a help she would have been to her brother—just what he needs—he craves companionship so much. What a comfort she would have been to Mamma, no doubt she would have saved Mamma this long and expensive trip to Shanghai, for with such a dear little son and daughter to make home happy, no matter how hard Mamma worked, her head would not have given out this way. Perhaps it is because Mamma is not feeling well, but somehow the loss of her little daughter grows harder and harder to bear. Oh, that she might come boldly to the throne of grace and find help in time of need knowing as the text says, "We have not a high priest which cannot be touched with the feeling of our infirmities."[120]

Not long after writing this Mamma had such a nice talk with dear Mrs. Fitch of Shanghai. She seems to have gotten into perfect harmony with God and his plans, and it makes Mamma long to do likewise; but so many times Mamma has earnestly tried to get in closer relations with God, and even with dear Papa's help never quite succeeded, that she finally thought it could not be for her, and that she must not covet such experiences, at least they were not for her yet— Mamma is so material, and these experiences seem to be for the more spiritual—our natures are not alike and we can't expect like experiences. Yet, Mamma can't help longing for a <u>happier</u>

---

[119] *David Harum: A Story of American Life* by Edward Noyes Wescott.
[120] Hebrews 4:15.

experience, and she has tried to lay her Isaac on the altar, and to let God do with her the best he can; and even where she may not have succeeded in this, it seems as if God himself <u>has taken</u> her most precious things, and she has tried to learn the lessons he would have her, and not be rebellious, but somehow as time goes on even the faint outlines that at first she thought she could discern of these lessons have grown dim, and more dim, and there has been no result, and of late rebellious feelings do arise sometimes, and she feels farther away than before these great losses came into her life. Something is wrong no doubt. Mrs. Fitch said that Mamma couldn't help feeling the heaviness of her losses, and neither could she expect to understand just how it could be better for her and Sherwood that Papa and Edith should be removed, but she must just give her feelings over to Jesus and trust him implicitly. Mamma has truly tried to do this, but as she told Mrs. Fitch it has been more because there seemed nothing else to do, in sort of a stoical way, not counting it a privilege so to do, in this particular loss, and secretly feeling that she could have trusted him better if he had not taken her precious ones away. Now this is a plain fact we fear, though very unbecoming of a Christian and a missionary to say. Mamma has been trying to examine her heart, it is hard to diagnose one's own case, but one trouble seems to be that she can't quite bring herself where she <u>wants</u> to feel that these losses were best. Sometimes, a long way off, she has thought it might be beautiful to feel

> "He emptied my hands of my treasured store,
> And His covenant love revealed,
> There was not a wound in my aching heart,
> But the balm of His breath hath healed."[121]

But somehow as yet she can't <u>will</u> to have those wounds closed; it would seem like forgetting her dear ones. So foolish as it may seem, and shortsighted as no doubt later it will look even to her, she goes on hugging those wounds, really refusing to have them healed! though up to the present she has never quite realize it. Putting it into words makes it seem worse. If God were to heal those wounds in spite of herself, and she could trustfully say the above, she realizes it would be blessed; but for herself to <u>will </u>it seems, somehow, she knows not how to express the <u>feeling</u>, but in cold words something like sacrifice! This is a clear state of feeling to be in, the more she thinks of it the more foolish it seems, for she knows those very loved ones would not have it for a moment, as much as Papa loved Mamma he desired her soul's good above all; poor stupid Mamma, she knows she has grown very dull of late—it has been all work and no play—and promises to continue to be. Something must be done. May God continue to have mercy on her, may his Holy Spirit teach her and bring her out of this low spiritual state.

---

[121] From "Retrospection" by Anna Shipton (1815-1901).

"Thou hast chastised me, and I was chastised, as a bullock unaccustomed to the yoke; turn thou me, and I shall be turned; for thou art the Lord my God."[122]

---

[122] Jeremiah 31:18.

Journal of Edith Margaret Hall

Edith Margaret Hall's Expenses

1895

Horlicks Food, malted milk and condensed milk	25.00
First short clothes and some sewing	4.00
3 pairs baby shoes (2 No. 1's and 1 No. 2)	0.85
3 pairs baby stockings	0.60
5 nursing bottles and 1 box nipples	0.75
Nursery pins (0.50), baby hair brush (0.20), graham crackers (0.40)	1.10
Hired help	96.00
Total	128.30

Presents

1 pair baby socks from Mrs. Reynolds of Korea
Knit cap of blue and white worsted, knit on The China by Miss Barton
Light blue lined with white "eider down" carriage blanket, Mrs. Young
Drawn-work linen trimming from Mrs. Noble
Light blue cashmere for a dress from Grandma Hall
Cambria and lace for apron from Aunt Alice
Brown gingham dress from Aunt Emma
Rattle from Joe, cloth dog from Yousanie
Box graham crackers from Aunt Annie

1896

1 pair shoes 3½ Jan. 18	0.25	
2 under waists size 2	0.70	
4 knit wool shirts	1.75	
1 pair stocking supporters	0.20	
Knit doll and rattle Feb. 18	0.30	
Syrup of Figs	0.40	
3 shirts	1.05	
1 Bonnet, white muslin, embroidered	0.98	
2 knit under-waists	0.50	
1 white dress embroidered short sleeves	1.74	
1 pink chamber dress	0.79	
3 yards ribbon (0.30), safety pins (0.25)	0.50	
1 Bonnet, brown silk a plush winter		2.75
1 brown cashmere dress	2.59	
1 brown and black heavy winter cloak	3.25	
2 wool shirts	1.18	
1 pair shoes	1.50	

4 pairs drawers	2.00
1 gingham dress	0.59
Safety pins	0.30
Kid crimpers	0.10
2 pairs drawers at 0.69	1.38
High chair	0.90
Rocking chair	0.35
Board for July, Aug., Sept. at Grandma's	6.00
Medicine	0.50
Help up to Nov.	75.00
Total	107.65

1897

2 gingham aprons	0.70
1 spring jacket (reefer)	1.49
1 drab cotton dress	0.98
1 pink cashmere	1.98
1 pair shoes 7½ at Liberty	0.70
To Mrs. Bosworth for care in N.Y.	2.00
2 pairs stockings	0.50
14 weeks board to Uncle Walter	14.00
1 pair shoes from N.Y. City 7½	1.35
Straw hat in Letcher (0.25), night knit clothes in Brockville (1.50)	1.75
Medicine in Letcher	0.50
Board on cars from St. Paul to Vancouver	0.52
Tips on steamer	1.00
¼ fare on Empress of India	40.00
Vaccine	1.00
Jinrikisha rides in Japan	0.50
Board in Japan	2.00
At Steward's, fuel and ranges and *yak*[123]	1.50
Freight and duty and expenses en route	5.00
At Söul, coolie line for rickshaw to January	0.25
¼ of 2 shares November Household account, fuel supply etc.	13.15
¼ of 2 shares San Francisco order bill (1/18 of whole order)	3.10
¼ of 2 shares England order (1/18 of whole order)	3.03
¼ of 2 shares Chicago order (1/18 of whole order)	7.82
¼ of 2 shares December Household account	4.33
Toys from Japan	1.00
Total	123.55

---

[123] Medicine in Korean.

Journal of Edith Margaret Hall

Presents from January 18, 1897 – January 18, 1898

1 small silver spoon from Mrs. Jones
2 pairs stockings from Aunt Kit
Candles and nuts from Jennie Intemann
25 cents from Dr. Pack
$1 from Mrs. Hanna
$1 from Grandma Hall
$1 from Grandma Sherwood, and pocket book and handkerchiefs
1 plate from Vira Powell (broken in January 1898)
1 glass cup from Joe and handkerchief, nuts and candy
Gum from Aunt Emma
1 doll from Nellie and 1 from Cousin Maud (both second hand), gone by end of year
1 small doll at Christmas pie, and ball.
1 set Japanese dishes
1 Japanese [toy] house
1 nice large doll from Gretchen Jones
Picture books from Mrs. Scranton and
1 handkerchief from Miss Rothweiler
1 rag doll at New Year's time
 Victoria Jubilee handkerchief from Aunt Jane
White apron from Aunt Alice
1 apron from Esther

Expenses 1898

Blue cloth dress (2.00) Trimmings and making (1.00)	Gold 2.00
No. 9 shoes from N. Y.	1.50
Repairs on shoes at Japanese shoemaker	0.35
1 chair and repairs on high chair	1.00
1 blue lawn and 1 red lawn dress with making	3.00
2 gingham aprons	0.30
Board and help ¼ of 2 shares to April 30	25.00
Fare to Pyong Yang and expenses on way	3.50
Paid for drugs etc.	7.50
Cheese cloth, used mostly as bibs and napkins	2.00
Coffin (silk and lawn 7 yen, lumber 2.40 yen)	5.00
Outer sealed box	1.50
Transfer to Seoul	17.00
Interment	2.50

Presents January 18, 1898 – January 18m 1899

1 pair shoes from Mrs. Appenzeller 7½

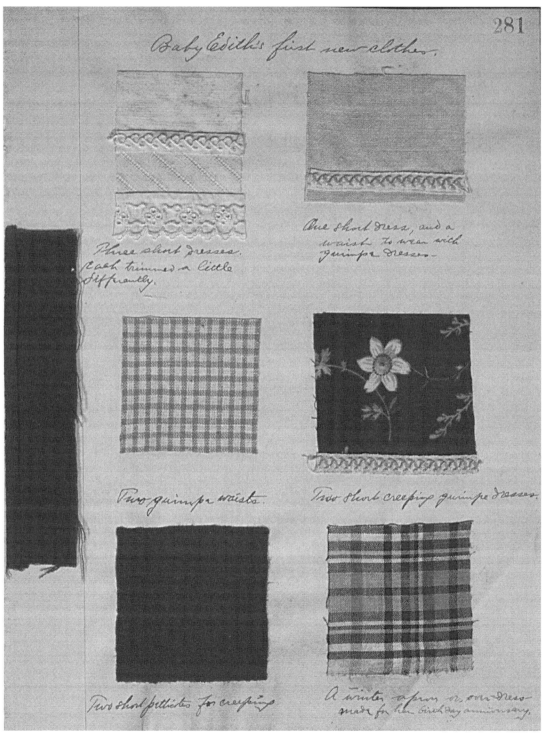

Baby Edith's first new clothes

Baby's Clothes

Softest linen and snowiest lawn,
With fairy fluting of lace;
'Broidery fine as the penciled fern
The fingers of frost-king trace;
Singing she sews the tiniest seam
While the garment grows apace.
A, the sweetest work a mother knows
Is making the baby's dainty clothes.

Her thoughts reach out across the years,
Losing herself in a dream;
A hope is set with the stitches fine
Of every delicate seam
An airy castle with turrets high
Stands in a golden gleam,
Ah, the dearest work a mother knows
Is making the baby's dainty clothes.

Appendix 1

The Sherwood's Farm Photo Postcard, Pleasant Drive, Liberty, New York[124]

This is presumed to be taken some time prior to 1952 before the postage increased from 1 cent to 2 cents. On the photo, Rosetta's son Sherwood Hall typed, "Ave. of Maples set out by my Grandfather about 1850 thru the old Homestead."

---

[124] Keepsakes from the Hall Family.

Appendix 2

Photo Collection of Rosetta Sherwood Hall in Pyongyang

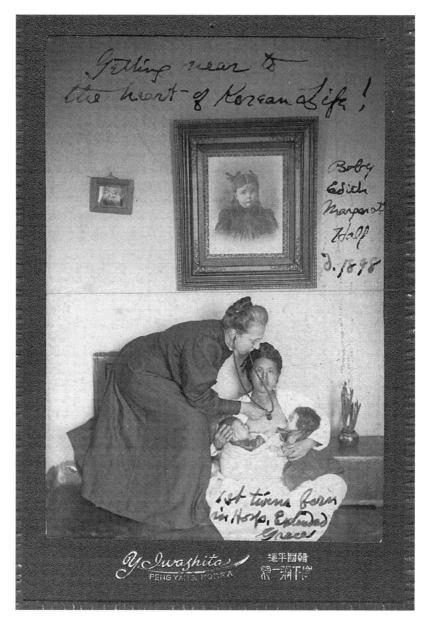

"Getting near to the heart of Korean Life!"
"Baby Edith Margaret Hall, d. 1898." Edith's picture at 2¼ years old.
"First twins born in the new Hospital of Extended Grace to Women & Children, Pyong Yang."

"Korean mother, Mrs. Do, with twin babies & older daughter, in the 'Edith Margaret Children's Ward.' Both [babies] lived to walk, but son died later. Daughter living. Sister Danshiree."

"A group of patients in the Waiting Room of Dispensary for Women & Children.
Hospital of Extended Grace, Pyong Yang, Korea"

Rosetta wrote in regards to the frame hung on the wall: "One paper framed contains the Governor's letter that he wrote when he bestowed the name on our Medical Plant and the other contains the letter written at the time the Emperor gave the 200 yen donation."

"Pyong Yang Department in Medicine for Women, November 1912"

"Refused admission in Severance Union Medical College,
But were later admitted into the Government Medical College"

Department of Medicine for Women, Pyong Yang, 1912

"A poor picture of the Pyong Yang Medical Class taken in Dr. Hall's Study."

"3 Graduate Nurses (Korean)"

"Nurses Martha & Grace were the first to graduate.
Then there was the sister of Alice Chyong, 'Nurse Ellen'— she is now nursing at Severance.
And I think Nurse Hope was the 4th,
but Dr. Cutler can tell you better or Mrs. Edmunds Harrison."

By courtesy of American Review of Reviews.

A Supper Party at "the Point," Pyong Yang, Korea, given by Governor Matsunaga to the First Convention in the Far East of Educators of the Blind and Deaf. See Review of Reviews, December, 1914.

First Convention in the Far East of Education of the Blind and Deaf, 1914.

Rosetta is sitting in the center of the front row

"A Grateful Patients" of with Dr. Rosetta Hall and her assistants, Pyong Yang 1917.
Rosetta in the center
Mrs. We-Sang Yi (Mrs. Grace We-Sang Yi) on the left back row
Miss Chu on the right back row
Mrs. Yun of We Ju second right on the front row
Mrs. Yun the Bible woman on the left front row.

"A group of 'grateful patients' – all gynaecological, who desired their pictures taken with Dr. Hall & her Korean assistants before she left Pyong Yang to take up the work at E. Gate, Soul in Sept. 1917.
Mrs. Yun, Bible woman.
Mrs. Lee, We-Sang, 1st Korean woman to receive Government license to practice medicine. She had been Dr. Hall's assistant for 5 yrs when the license law went into effect in Korea & men who had practiced 5 yrs or more were licensed without exam.
Dr. Rosetta Hall in Korean silk gown made for her by Mrs. Yun a g.p. [gynecological patient] from We Ju.
Mrs. Yun of We Ju, who later also donated 30 yen to the fund for educating
more Korean medical women.
Miss Chu, who now is the 1st woman student of dentistry, studying with a Japanese woman dentist who graduated in Phila., Pa. many years ago.
Mrs. Lee & Miss Chu were the faithful assistants of Dr. Hall at the time photo was taken."

Front row, Dr. Rosetta Hall and Mrs. Yun
Back row, Mrs. We-Sang Lee on the left and Miss Chu on the right.

To identify the individuals on the photo, Rosetta wrote on the back:

"Miss Chu, now studying Dentistry & Pharmacy, Sŏul.

Mrs. Grace Yi, We-Sang
Mrs. Yun, the G. P. (gynecological patient) who presented the silk gown,
also paid medical student fund. Also wrote her gratitude in her own blood.
Dr. Hall"

Pyong Yang Blind and Deaf School

Front row left to right: Chyo Fanny's mother, Mrs. Chun
Back row left to right: Mrs. Shin-Myong Pak, Syong-Sil Kim, Miss Il-Shim Pak, Fanny Cho

Timeline of Dr. Rosetta Sherwood Hall
(1865 – 1951)

1865	9.19	Born in Liberty, New York
		Mother: Phoebe Gildersleeve Sherwood
		Father: Rosevelt Rensler Sherwood
1876		Graduates from Chestnut Ridge Primary School
1880		Graduates from Liberty Normal Institute
1881	9	Enters Liberty Normal Institute's "Teacher's Class"
	10	Obtains Second Grade Teacher's Certificate[125]
1882	2.6	Transfers to Montgomery Union School, following her for-Mer professor Mr. Reuben Fraser[126], newly appointed Principal of the school
	4	Graduates from Montgomery Union School
	5.1	Starts teaching at Huntington District School
	9.6	Enters the Oswego State Normal School
1883		Graduates from the Oswego State Normal School; obtains a First Grade Teacher's Certificate; teaches at Bethel District School
1884		Teaches at Chestnut Ridge School, Sullivan County, New York
1886		Enters the Woman's Medical College of Pennsylvania
1889	3.14	Graduates from the Woman's Medical College of Pennsylvania
		Interns at the Nursery and Children's Hospital, Staten Island

---

[125] By the time Rosetta was teaching, a first grade certificate was good for 2 years, a second grade certificate good for eighteen months, and third grade certificate good for 12 months.

[126] Professor Reuben Fraser was Principal of the Liberty Normal Institute when Rosetta entered the school, but when the Montgomery Academy merged with a public school in 1882 and became the Montgomery Union School, he took the position of Principal.

	11	Works as a physician for the New York Deaconess Home
		Begins medical missionary work in Hell's Kitchen in New York City; meets her future husband Rev. William James Hall, M.D. (b. January 16, 1860, Glen Buell, Ontario, Canada), who is in charge of the medical missionary work in the slums of New York
1890	8.21	Leaves Liberty, New York for Korea as a medical missionary, under the auspices of the Woman's Foreign Missionary Society of the Methodist Episcopal Church
	9.4	Boards the *S.S. Oceanic* in San Francisco
	9.24	Arrives in Yokohama
	10.10	Arrives in Pusan, Korea
	10.13	Arrives in Chemulpo, Korea
	10.14	Arrives in Seoul
	10.15	Starts medical work at Po Ku No Kwan, the firs Woman's Hospital and Dispensary established by the Methodist Episcopal Mission
	10.24	Selects two girls from the Ehwa-Haktang Mission School, O Waka San and Chom Tong Kim, for medical assistance training
1891	1.25	Chom-Tong is baptized as "Esther"
	1	Starts teaching physiology to five girls: Esther, O Waka San, Susanna, Pong Sun ("Mary Sparks Wheeler"), and Annie
	8.21	Travels to Chefoo, China, with Miss Bengel
	12.15	William James Hall arrives in Korea (Pusan) as a medical missionary for the Methodist Episcopal Church
1892	3	William goes on a country trip with George Heber Jones; visits Pyongyang for the first time
	6.27	Rosetta marries William James Hall
	7	Returns to Seoul from a honeymoon in Chefoo
	9	William is appointed to Pyongyang; Rosetta is appointed to Seoul

1893	3.15	Opens the East Gate Dispensary (Baldwin Dispensary) in Seoul
	5.24	Esther Kim marries Yousan Pak
	11.10	Rosetta and William's first son Sherwood is born in Seoul
1894	5.8	The Hall family arrives in Pyongyang with Esther and Yousan; begins medical work; begins instruction of the blind girl Pong-Nae O
	6.6	Evacuates to Seoul due to persecution
	8.1	Sino-Japanese War begins
	10.1	William leaves for Pyongyang
	11.19	William returns to Seoul, sick with typhus fever
	11.24	William dies
	12.10	Rosetta departs from Chemulpo to America with her son Sherwood and Esther and Yousan
	12.16	Arrives in Nagasaki
	12.18	Arrives in Kobe
	12.21	Boards the *S.S. China* in Yokohama for San Francisco
1895	1.6	Arrives in San Francisco
	1.14	Arrives in Liberty, New York
	1.18	Gives birth to Edith Margaret in Liberty, New York
	2	Esther Pak enters the Liberty Union School; Yousan works at the Sherwood Farm
	4	Begins a biography of her late husband and fundraises for the establishment of the Hall Memorial Hospital in Pyongyang

	6.27	Rosetta's father Rosevelt R. Sherwood dies
	8	Rosetta visits her husband's family in Glen Buell, Ontario with her children and Esther and Yousan
	9	Esther Pak enters the Nursery and Children's Hospital of New York City; also studies for admission into the medical school
	10	Rosetta attends the Annual Meeting of the New York Branch of the Woman's Foreign Missionary Society (W.F.M.S.) in Brooklyn, October 16-18; visits Esther Pak at the hospital
1896	2	Visits New York and Middletown
	4	Attends a conference for the International Medical Missionary Society (I.M.S.S.), New York City
	5	Moves residence to 121 E. 45th Street with children and Yousan
	6	Moves into the New York Deaconess Home for work; sends children back to Liberty; Yousan takes a new job for the family of Rev. A.B. Sanford in New York
	6.22	Begins work at the New York Deaconess Home; works as the examining physician for the Christian Herald Fresh-Air Children Summer Camp at Mt. Lawn, Nyack until September
	9	Esther Pak enters the Baltimore Woman's Medical College
	9.28	Rosetta works for the International Medical Missionary Society; moves back into 121 E. 45th Street residence with children
	10.28	Attends the General Executive meeting for the W.F.M.S. at Rochester, New York
1897	2.1	Establishment of the Hall Memorial Hospital in Pyongyang; Sherwood attends kindergarten until March
	5.20	Closes her work for I.M.M.S. at the Deaconess Home; decides to return to Korea
	5.22-30	Visits Esther Pak in Baltimore
	5.31	Arrives in Liberty, New York; finishes manuscripts of her husband's biography; Yousan also returns to Liberty to depart for Korea

	8	Publishes *The Life of Rev. William James Hall, M.D.*
		Yousan decides not to return to Korea and gets a new job at Mrs. Adgate's house, near the Sherwood farm
	9.6	Rosetta leaves Liberty for Korea with Sherwood and Edith Margaret; visits husband's family in Glen Buell, Ontario en-route to Korea
	10.11	Boards the *S.S. Empress of India* in Vancouver
	11.10	Arrives in Chemulpo
		Makes the first embossed book for the blind of Korea, pricked on oiled Korean mulberry paper by hand
1898	4.29	Leaves Seoul to start work in Pyongyang
	5.1	Arrives in Pyongyang
	5.23	Edith Margaret dies of dysentery
	6.18	Opens the Women's Dispensary of Extended Grace in Pyongyang, as well as the Mother-Baby Clinic and the School for the Blind
1899	5	Attends the Annual Meeting in Seoul; embarks on a building project of the Edith Margaret Children's Wards
1900	1	The School for the Blind is built
	4.28	Yousan Pak dies in Baltimore of tuberculosis
	5.5	Rosetta's mother Phoebe G. Sherwood dies
	5	Esther Pak receives M.D. degree
	10	Esther Pak arrives in Korea
1901	3	Due to overwork, Rosetta recuperates in Chemulpo and Seoul
	5	Attends Annual Meeting in Seoul
	6.7	Departs for America with Sherwood

	6.22	Boards the *S.S. Nippon Maru* in Yokohama
	7.7	Arrives in San Francisco
	7	Arrives in Castile, New York
	8	Enters the Castile Sanatorium and stays for 8 months
	10	Attends the New York Branch Annual Meeting
1902	4.5	Discharged from the Sanatorium; moves to Brother Charles' home
	8.14	Leaves Liberty for Korea (via Europe)
	8.25	Visits husband's family in Canada for one week
	9.2	Boards the *S.S. St. Paul* in New York
	9.10	Arrives in London
	10.16	Boards the *S.S. Glen Logan* from Swansea to Batúm
1903	3.18	Arrives in Seoul, Korea
		Works at the Women's Hospital of Extended Grace in Pyongyang with Esther Pak
1906	11	The Women's Hospital of Extended Grace in Pyongyang is burnt down
1908	9	The new Women's Hospital of Extended Grace in Pyongyang is built
		Sherwood completes the eighth grade at Pyongyang Foreign School and enters the Chefoo Boarding School
1909		Rosetta opens the Pyongyang School for the Deaf
1910	4.13	Esther Pak dies of tuberculosis
	6	Rosetta attends the Edinburgh World Missionary Conference as a delegate from Korea, and then takes a furlough in America

1911	4	Sherwood enrolls at the Mount Hermon School in Massachusetts
		Rosetta completes her furlough and returns to Korea
1912	3	Starts a Medical Training Class in Pyongyang with Mary Cutler, M.D.
1914	8	Enrolls three female students as auditors at the Government Medical School in Seoul: Soo-Kyong Ahn, Hae-Ji Kim, and Young-Heung Kim
		The First Annual Convention on the Education of the Blind And Deaf of the Far East is held in Pyongyang, August 11-14
1915		Sherwood enters Mount Union College in Alliance, Ohio
1917		Rosetta moves to Seoul; works at the East Gate Woman's Hospital and Dispensary
1918		Takes a furlough; works as a physician for the Board of Health in Philadelphia; Sherwood is engaged to Marian Bottomley
		The three female students at the Government School obtain medical licenses
1920		Rosetta starts a Woman's Medical Training Class in Seoul
	9	Marian Bottomley enters the Woman's Medical College of Pennsylvania
1921		Rosetta serves as the director of the East Gate Woman's Hospital and Dispensary
		Opens a Women's Hospital in Chemulpo
1922	6.21	Sherwood and Marian Bottomley are married in Ohio
1923		Sherwood graduates from the Medical College at the University of Toronto
1924	6	Marian Bottomley graduates from the Woman's Medical College of Pennsylvania

1925	8.15	Sherwood and his wife leave for Korea
1927	2.18	Rosetta's grandson William James Hall is born
1928	9.4	The Woman's Medical Training Class in Seoul becomes the Kyong-Sung Woman's Medical Institute
	10.28	Sherwood opens the Haiju School of Hygiene for the Tuberculosis
1932	10.8	Second grandson Joseph Keightley is born
	12.3	Sherwood prints the first Christmas Seal (1932-1933) in Korea
1933	9.23	The Haiju Sanatorium dedicates its chapel to Rosetta
	11	The Woman's Medical Institute graduates its first students
	11.25	Retires from the mission field; returns to America to take care of Brother Frank Sherwood in Groversville, New York
1934	9.12	Granddaughter Phyllis Marian is born
1936		Opens a medical practice in Groversville, New York
1938		Returns to Liberty and opens a medical practice
1943		Retires from medicine; moves to the Bancroft-Taylor Rest Home in Ocean Grove, New Jersey
1951	4.5	Dies in Ocean Grove, New Jersey. Ashes are interred at Yanghwajin Foreign Missionary Cemetery in Seoul

Index

A Cradle Hymn, 14
Abbott, Edgar W., 34
Adgate, Mrs., 45
Aldrich, Thomas Bailey, 82
Amah, 57, 58, 60, 63
Appenzeller, Henry G., 84
Appenzeller, Mary, 56, 57, 98
Aromatic Spirits of Ammonia, 63
Athens High School, 47
Baby Bell, 82
Baby's Clothes, 105
Baird, William B., 84
Barton, Laura J., 10, 101
Beers, Ethel Lynn, 11
Bickfort, Nancy, 19
Binghamton, 20
Bismuth, 64, 65, 66, 67, 68, 69
Bolton, Abram, 19
Bolton, Benjamin[1], 19
Bolton, Benjamin[2], 19
Bolton, Caroline, 19
Bolton, George, 19
Bolton, Henry (Uncle Henry), 19
Bolton, Jane, 19
Bolton, John (great-Grandfather Bolton), 19, 47
Bolton, Martha, 19
Bolton, Mrs. Alice Colborne, 19
Bolton, Mrs. Martha Elliott, 19
Bolton, Nancy, 19
Bolton, Rebecca, 19
Bolton, Sarah (Aunt Sarah), 19
Bolton, Sarah[1], 19
Bolton, Susan, 19
Bolton, William (Uncle William), 19, 47
Bolton, William[1], 19
Bolton, William[2], 19
Bonney, Mrs. Elizabeth Gildersleeve, 20
Bonney, Seth, 20
Bovanine, 69, 72, 74, 75
Brockville, 23, 46, 47, 56, 102
Brooklyn, 22
Brown, Helen E., 95
Browning, Elizabeth Barret, 39, 56
Bryan, Mary, 46
Burr, Mrs. Polly Sherwood, 10
Caldwell, Dr., 22
Calomel, 62
Camphor, 73
Canadian Pacific Railway (C.P.R.), 49
Carbolic Acid, 69, 71, 72
Carlton Junction, 47
Carrie, Mrs. Alice Bolton, 19
catarrhal pneumonia, 52, 54, 55, 89
Chemulpo, 52, 55, 58, 89
Chloroanodyne, 64, 65, 66
Christian Herald Children's Home (C.H.C.H.), 38
Clayton, Mr. and Mrs., 22
Crary, Horace H., 10
Crary, Mrs. Polly Burr, 10, 20, 90
Crummy, William James, 28
David Haum: A Story of American Life, 98
digitalis, 53
Dover's powder, 65, 66
Dowkoutt, George D., 26
Drew Theological Seminary, 28
dysentery, 11, 12, 17, 19, 49, 52, 64
Edith Margaret Children's Wards, 89, 93, 96, 97
Field, Eugene, 14, 32
Fitch, Mrs., 98, 99
Follwell, E. Douglas, 65, 66, 67, 72, 77
Forester, Fanny, 8
Gilroy, Mr., 47
Glen Buell, 18, 28
Glycerine, 73
Gray, Allan, 46
Gray, Harry, 46
Gray, Mrs. Alice Hall (Aunt Alice), 13, 20, 46, 47, 101, 103
Gray, William (Uncle Will Gray), 46
Hall, Boyd, 47

Hall, Edith Margaret
   1 year, 29, 30
   16 months, 36
   2.5 years, 42
   4 months, 15
   6 months, 17
   8 months, 22
   arrival to Korea, 52
   arrival to Yokohama, 51
   at Grandpa Hall's, 18, 47
   at Uncle Frank's, 16
   birth, 8
   birthplace, 7
   burial, 84
   catarrhal pneumonia, 52
   death, 75, 77
   dysentery, 12, 64
   Edith Margaret Children's Wards, 89
   funeral service, 81
   house where she passed away, 80
   in Liberty, NY, 11, 14, 15, 16, 21, 25, 32
   in Seoul, 56
   letter to Mamma, 44
   letters from Grandma Sherwood, 79
   memorial birthday parties for Korean girls, 93, 95
   memorial service, 89
   Rubeola (measles), 62
   second birthday, 40
   third birthday, 56
   to Korea, 44, 45, 49
   visit to Uncle David Powell's, 48
Hall, George (Grandpa Hall), 10, 18
Hall, James (Uncle James), 18
Hall, John (Uncle John), 18
Hall, Lillie, 10, 47
Hall, Mrs. Margaret Bolton (Grandma Hall), 10, 13, 18, 19, 20, 47, 101, 103
Hall, Mrs. Rosetta Sherwood, M.D.
   annual meeting, NY Branch W.F.M.S., 22
   arrival to Korea, 52
   at 121 E. 45th St., NY, 40
   at Brother Frank's, 16
   at Shanghai, 98
   birth of daughter, 8
   Christian Herald Fresh-Air Children camp, Mt. Lawn, 38
   daughter's memorial, 89
   death of daughter Edith Margaret, 75, 77
   I.M.M.S. meeting, 31, 33, 36
   in Glen Buell, Canada, 18, 47
   in Liberty, NY, 11, 14, 15, 25, 30
   in Seoul, 56
   letter from Rev. Appenzeller, 84
   letter from Rev. Powell, 96
   letters from Esther Pak, 26
   letters from Mother, 50, 59, 60
   memorial writing of Dr. William James Hall, 26
   return to Korea, 44, 45, 49, 51
   telegram from W.F.M.S., 80
   third wedding anniversary, 17
   visit to daugter's grave, 95
   visit to the Powell's, 48
Hall, Rev. William James, M.D., 18, 19
   childhood, 28
   death, 26, 27
Hall, Sherwood
   arrival to Korea, 52
   at Grandpa Hall's, 18, 47
   at Shanghai, 98
   at Uncle Frank's, 16
   in Liberty, NY, 8, 12, 14, 15, 25, 29, 35
   in Seoul, 57
   return to Korea, 44, 45, 49, 51
   visit to Papa and sister's graves, 95
   visit to Uncle David Powell's, 48
Han River, 26
Hang Up the Baby's Stocking, 24
Harris, Lillian N., 49, 58, 68
Harum, David, 98
Hayes, William James, 28
Holm, Saxe, 87
Horlick's Food, 12, 16, 66, 67, 68, 69, 70, 71, 72, 101
Horn, Mr., 43
Hulbert, Madeline, 56
Hypoderm, 67, 68, 70, 71
If I Could Keep Her So, 9
International Medical Missionary Society (I.M.M.S.), 36

Jesus Loves Me, 82, 96
Johnson, Emily Bugbee, 45
Jone, Mrs. Margaret Bengel, 47
Jones, Gretchen. *See* Jones, Margaret Jane
Jones, Margaret Jane (Gretchen), 45, 47, 49, 50, 54, 57, 98, 103
Jones, Mrs. Margaret Bengel, 47, 48, 49, 50, 54, 59, 103
Judson, Emily E., 8
Kim, Chang Sik, 84
Kumyongie, 69
Landis, Dr., 53, 54
Lee, Graham, 84
Lee, Mrs. Graham, 80
Liberty, NY, 7, 9, 10, 14, 15, 16, 17, 21, 38, 45, 57, 58, 102
Longfellow, Henry Wadsworth, 10
Lyn, 19, 20
Mellin's Food, 64, 65
Miller, Emily Huntington, 24
Miller, Noland, 56
Moffett, Samuel A., 26, 27
Mother Truth's Melodies: Common Sense for Children, A Kindergarten, 9
Moulton, Louisa Chandler, 9
Mount Lawn, 38
Muzzy, Alice, 35
My Baby, 87
My Bird, 8
Nagasaki, 51
Naylor, Lizzie
   see Sandford, Mrs. Bruce, 14
Nettie (Amah), 60, 70
New Dublin, 19
New York Deaconess Home, 46
Noble, Mrs. Mattie Wilcox, 82, 98, 101
Noble, Ruth, 93, 98
Noble, William Arthur, 27, 76, 81, 84
Northville, NY, 16
Nursery and Child's Hospital of New York City, 21
Ode to a Baby, 35
Ogdensburg, NY, 45
Pak, Esther, 8, 10, 15, 16, 20, 22, 26, 103
   Nursery and Child's Hospital, NY City, 21, 22
   public school, Liberty, NY, 10, 11

Pak, Yousan, 10, 15, 16, 22, 25, 31, 33, 37, 38, 42, 45, 54, 58, 68, 76, 79, 101
Parker, Mrs., 22
Percival, Mr., 47
Percival, Mrs. Sarah Hall (Aunt Sarah Percival), 18
Pierce, Nellie, 49, 84
Powell, David M., 48, 96
Powell, Jason Gould (Cousin Jason), 48, 49
Powell, Mrs. Adaline Annette Sherwood, 48
Powell, Vira (Coousin Vira), 48
Pyong Yang, 14, 26, 27, 64, 80, 84, 89, 98, 103
quinine, 54, 58, 61, 70, 72, 73, 74
Reynolds, Mrs. William D., 9, 101
Roosa, John, M.D., 45
Rothweiler, Louise C., 57, 63, 103
Rowsom, Mrs. Jane Bolton (Aunt Jane), 47, 56, 103
Rowsom, Rebecca, 28
Rubeola, 62
S.S. China, 10
S.S. Empress of India, 44, 49, 102
S.S. Hai Riong, 64
S.S. Hiego Maru, 51
S.S. The Island Belle, 46
Saint Lawrence River, 46
Sandford, Mrs. Bruce, 14
Sangster, Margaret E., 95
Santonin, 62
Sarles, Leslie, 16
Sarles, Mrs., 15
Scranton, PA, 20
Seoul, 27, 55, 59, 64, 84, 95, 102
Shanghai, 98
Sherwood, Annie (Aunt Annie), 29, 36, 37, 38, 43, 48, 79, 101
Sherwood, Charles Hurd, 20, 45
Sherwood, Clarence MacKinlay (Cousin Clare), 18, 25
Sherwood, Fanny, 10
Sherwood, Frank R. (Uncle Frank), 16, 18, 19, 25, 38
Sherwood, Lena (Cousin Lena), 20
Sherwood, Mrs. Catherine Anne MacKinlay (Aunt Kit), 18, 103

Sherwood, Mrs. Emma C. Tice (Aunt Emma), 25, 29, 101, 103
Sherwood, Mrs. Margaret Ver Noy (Aunt Maggie), 9, 10, 25
Sherwood, Mrs. Rosevelt R. (Grandma Sherwood), 11, 17, 19, 21, 22, 36, 37, 40, 42, 48, 50, 60, 79, 93, 103
Sherwood, Nellie (Coousin Nellie), 29
Sherwood, Rev. Frank R., 36
Sherwood, Rosevelt R. (Grandpa Sherwood), 11, 17, 26
Sherwood, Rosevelt Rensler (Cousin Velt), 9, 18, 25
Sherwood, Walter, Jr., 29
Sherwood, William Fanton, 57, 60
Smith, May Riley, 91, 92
Some Time, 92
Söul. *See* Seoul
Spts. Frumenti, 64, 65, 66, 68, 69, 70, 75
Syrup of Figs, 26, 53, 62, 63, 101
The ABC of Animals, 25
The Other One, 29
The Personal Life of David Livingstone, 25
There is a Happy Land, 96

Thorn, Mrs., 45
Tourisse, Mr., 47
Tr. Ferri Chlor., 73
Traslow, Mrs. John, 22
Turpentine, 74
Valentine's beef juice, 65, 67, 68, 69, 70
Vancouver, 49, 52, 102
Watts, Isaac, 14
We Shall Sleep But Not Forever, 84
Webster, Dr., 14
Weighing the Baby, 11
Wells, James Hunter, 65, 66, 77
Wescott, Edward Noyes, 98
White-Clovers and White-Dandelions, 95
Wilson, Joe (Josiah), 19, 31, 37, 38, 40, 45, 58, 60, 76, 79, 89, 101, 103
With Stethoscope in Asia: Korea, 21
Woman's Foreign Missionary Society (W.F.M.S.), 22, 49, 55, 60, 80
Yokohama, 51
Young, Louise, 90
Young, Mrs. Emma Crary, 10, 90
Young, Polly, 90

From the Hall Family

On behalf of the Hall family and our parents, Dr. Edward and Phyllis (Hall) King, whose final project together was to donate Dr. Rosetta Sherwood Hall's six preserved diaries of medical missionary work in Korea, and to see them transcribed and translated so that her inspirational story could be shared with the Korean people and the world, we are delighted to witness the completion of their publication. We would like to thank Dr. Hyun Sue Kim, Esther Foundation and Yanghwajin for all the hours of hard work, dedication and love to see this project come to fruition. The Korean people have always shown respect for their history and honor and affection to the Hall family, and we share that fondness for them as well. We pray that the readers of the Rosetta Diaries would be blessed by these stories of loving faith and service to our Lord and Savior and thus be encouraged to serve Him as well.

Clifford King

Marcia (King) Everett

Laurie (King) Skipper

Children of Dr. Edward and Phyllis (Hall) King

Grandchildren of Drs. Sherwood and Marian Hall

Great-Grandchildren of Drs. William James and Rosetta Sherwood Hall

Afterword

At the conclusion of the three-year journey of translating Dr. Rosetta Sherwood Hall's diaries into Korean, I was asked to write an afterword. When I visited Dr. Edward King and his wife Phyllis (Hall) King at their home in McLean, VA in January 2015, we had no idea how this project would carry on. Neither did I know how this work would impact me. I can proclaim now that God's faithfulness has completed the good work He has begun on us! Not only the six volumes of Rosetta's diaries are beautifully published but also I was created into a new being. I praise Him for His faithfulness, patiently teaching me through Rosetta's story "the ways of His statutes" (Psalm 119:33) and giving me understanding.

I grew up in the Korean countryside of Moongyeong, a daughter of humble Christian farmer. After school, I would stop by the village church to pray and then would lead our family's ox to the mountains to graze until dusk. While it chomped on weeds, I pondered my future and who I was to become. I wanted to pass the big test and go to the city school, and then I would become His servant. As I pulled on the rope to ring the church bell before the church services, my little body would swing up higher and higher to that dream.

I never had to worry about how I was going to get into that big-city high school. When I was in the eighth grade, my family immigrated to the United States, sponsored by an aunt, a nurse who had settled in Phoenix, Arizona. My family worked in menial jobs to pay for our living, and when I was ninth grade, I lived in my father's boarding house, caring for senior citizens, cutting their hair, feeding them and making sure they took their medicine. I did that until I entered college.

A fourth-generation Christian, my original dream was to be a medical evangelist like the one who had served in the hometown church my grandfather had built. The Presbyterian nurse had been the main health care provider for the town's people. When I was accepted to medical school, this dream seemed to be at my reach;

however, becoming a wife and mother altered everything. The imminent needs were at home, with children and family.

By the time I encountered the diaries of Dr. Rosetta Hall, I was in great despair. My marriage was falling apart. Although I was the "supermom" who kept up a full time career while raising two children, and even doing humanitarian works like going to short-term medical mission trips, the very core of the family was destroyed. I felt like a failure and there was nothing I could do. Transcribing Rosetta's diaries during this time was the best remedy God had provided for me. There was a revival in my heart, which gradually transformed me into a new being.

As Rosetta left her hometown for Korea, I became Rosetta. I journeyed with her through the land and sea and met strange people. But those strange people became me, the poor and ignorant. I became the woman restricted by the Confucian Law and the underprivileged. Rosetta came to me and lifted me to become Esther Pak, the first Korean woman physician trained in America. Rosetta opened my blind eyes and deaf ears and made me learn about the love of Christ.

I became Rosetta when she lost her husband and when she struggled to pursue her calling as a single mother of two children. My heart ached when she was unable to take care of her own children while caring for so many other people. I was devastated when her little daughter was taken away from her. I rebelled with her when she cried, "How can their removal be better for all of us, God?" I struggled with her to understand the meaning of the suffering. "Thou hast chastised me, and I was chastised, as a bullock unaccustomed to the yoke; turn thou me, and I shall be turned; for thou art the Lord my God." (Jeremiah 31:18) But at the end, by the Grace of God, we realized that "just putting all our feelings in Jesus and absolutely trusting Him" was the only way to conquer. We were saved by this great trial of faith. And I was assured that she, like her husband and daughter, received the blessing of "a worthy death in the sight of the Lord" (Psalm 116: 15) and entered into glory.

I truly wish the same blessings to all the readers. The six books of Rosetta Diary contain heartbreaking stories. There are some happy moments, but the death of William James Hall and the death of little Edith Margaret Hall overwhelms the whole atmosphere. Through spiritual eyes, I wish that every reader can see the fruits of the deaths of these two martyrs.

This work was possible because of collaboration and unity with our team: the Esther Foundation, the Yanghwajin Institute, the Hongsungsa, and the 100 Anniversary Memorial Church. I also thank Professor Frank P. Sherwood Hall for his book, *Changing America: Seen Through One Sherwood Family Line 1634-2006*, which was a very helpful resource. Most importantly, I cannot thank enough the Hall family for letting us share this great treasure with us. I believe that God will reward every one for all his/her hard work.

Hyun Sue Kim
October 19, 2017
Colorado Springs

Made in the USA
Middletown, DE
10 February 2022